FREE TO LIVE

ONE WOMAN'S JOURNEY THROUGH

ANOREXIA TO LIFE

JO LUHRS

ISBN 0-646-44481-6

Published by RNJ Resources

47 Yarramundi Drive, Dean Park NSW 2761

Front Cover design by Jo Luhrs and Michael Dias

Typesets in Garamond, and Calisto.

Printed by Booksurge.com.au

ACKNOWLEDGEMENTS

I would firstly like to acknowledge my Healer and Saviour, Jesus Christ, without whose intervention in my life at a point of great crisis I would not be here to tell of His wonders.

I thank my darling family, Richard, Deborah and Daniel for believing in me — not only to come through but to stand tall. Thanks for encouraging me with writing even though it seems to have taken forever.

Thanks Dad (who is now in Heaven with Jesus, cheering us on) and Mum for your Love and one of the great hallmarks of your lives — the never give up of faith – this I know was part of "the miracle". And for always being an inspiration to me.

Thank you to all those who have helped me pen and publish this book.

A special thanks to Michael Dias for incredible help with scanning and graphics — and Shaunaugh Cimarosti and Martine Williams and for helping with the editing of the manuscript.

FOREWORD *by Darlene Zschech*

Jo has been a member of the Worship and Creative Arts team which I oversee at Hillsong Church for the last six years. I have seen her faithfulness in the team and also the amazing way God has been able to work in her life.

I thank God for her willingness to write her very vulnerable story and her ability to share what may seem "raw", because this story is a story of grace, and it will bring hope.

I believe in God's love to take broken lives and restore them and turn these beautiful lives into trophies of grace.

Darlene Zschech

ENDORSEMENTS

Brian Houston – Senior Pastor Hillsong Church

Jo's story is an inspiration. She had the courage to face her challenge with anorexia and the faith to overcome it before it robbed her of her future. Her journey to health and wholeness is a great encouragement to others to stand up and choose life!

Christine Caine – Equip & Empower Ministries

I have known Jo and her family for many years. She is a woman who has broken free from her past and now stands to tell of God's grace in her life. I know this book will prove a great help for many who struggle to see themselves as God truly sees them.

Nancy Alcorn – Founder of Mercy Ministries Intl.

"*Free to Live* allows the reader to see inside the mind of a woman with an eating disorder and better understand the complexity of this problem. This book exposes the lies that so many women believe today about their image. I believe this is a powerful must-read for anyone who needs to know that it is possible to overcome an eating disorder and be completely free. I commend Jo for being so real and vulnerable in the hope that others will receive the help they so desperately need. Discover one woman's journey through *Free to Live* as she moves out of the tangled web of darkness and into the light of freedom and restoration."

CONTENTS

CHAPTER 1   WHO AM I?

I was born Jo-Ann Lee Cartledge on October 9, 1964, to adoring parents David and Marie Cartledge, and big brother David Jnr. We lived at the time in a small town called Devonport, which is in Tasmania where dad and mum were pastors of a small church.

It wasn't too much longer before we were joined by another little bundle, Nathan, and for quite a long time the three of us were like The Three Musketeers; we played, we fought, and had fun together — we had good times and bad times like any normal children.

We moved a few times, and then we eventually went to Townsville in North Queensland where we were to stay for many years.

It was great being the only girl, because although sometimes I would have loved to have a sister, I also loved being looked after by my brothers. I still remember vividly one day coming home from school with Dave, and I had been teased and picked on by a boy in my class, and Dave wouldn't stand for it — he gave the boy a lashing for treating his little sister like that.

After eight years dad and mum told us that we were going to have something special happen, and that someone was going to come and live with us.

I thought that maybe our Aunty Lil was coming to live with us. But none of us could guess the secret, that mum was going to have another baby, and this baby was Andrew. So Andrew completed our family, and he grew up with way too many dads and mums, but lots of love.

We had moved to Townsville because dad was going to be the new church minister there. I never had a problem with dad being a pastor or working for the church, because even from when I was a little girl I felt close to God and knew Him to be my friend. I was nine when I said to my mother one Sunday afternoon, "I want to go and receive the baptism of the Holy Spirit at church tonight". I'm sure my mother was taken aback by this statement coming from a child, and her response was "If that is what you want then you will have to do it on your own". So when the time came for church that night, we had a guest preacher — Pastor Norm Armstrong — and he gave a call for those who wanted to receive the Holy Spirit. I was the first person to respond, and received so simply, just like a waterfall bubbling upwards from my stomach. Pastor Norm said to remember to use the gift daily to talk to God, which I took very seriously. I would lie on my bed at night and speak in my new heavenly language to God.

When I was fourteen I was asked to work for the church as a junior secretary. This was a wonderful time of learning to work in a team. I loved my life, including the work — I was also in the church choir which was great, as I have always loved to sing. We were amazingly blessed to have many prominent visiting speakers stay in our home or visit our home for meals, which was a great privilege. I remember sitting on the lounge room floor with my brother and Dr Yonggi Cho looking at family albums. Another time we had had Barry Maguire doing a concert at our church, and my mother was sick and couldn't attend the concert, so when he came by our house to visit he played a little concert for mum in our lounge room — that was cool.

Two of my brothers struggled greatly for years with the issue of being preacher's kids, but they have now come to terms with this and are doing brilliantly. I saw things from such a different angle right from the start. I always felt it was such an honour, and we as kids got to meet some of God's special people because of their connection with our parents.

I never really struggled in my teen years with being rebellious as my brothers did, but in a way often felt the burden or responsibility of holding the family together, and being the good child. Although this was never expected by dad and mum, I nevertheless felt the responsibility within myself.

Right throughout my teens I never really had any relationships with boys apart from a few crushes and one two to three week long relationship with a boy when I was thirteen, which dissolved almost as fast as it began. I think most of the boys were dead scared of even broaching a relationship with me, because of whose daughter I was. So this was fine — I never really felt the need.

I worked for the church for several years, and then when I was eighteen I went to Bible College and continued to work part-time in the church office. I always had a desire for ministry in some shape or form.

It was within weeks that I was to meet the man of my dreams. Tall (192 cm — 6' 3½" on the old scale), dark and exquisitely handsome — Richard Michael Luhrs.   This was something very foreign to me — actually having great feelings for someone whom I could respect, who wasn't scared witless of my parents.

It wasn't too long before we started spending an awful lot of lunch breaks together and you could literally feel the rumours starting about us.

A few months later Rich went to see my dad about our relationship to see if dad and mum were okay about our friendship, about which my dad told him they were very happy. Then Rich and I started formally dating, which was great, as we both got on so well together. We are from different worlds, and have different personalities completely, but are a great balance to each other. Rich is quite carefree, optimistic, funny, jovial and everybody's friend; while I am more of a deep thinker, more quiet, melancholic, choleric and trying really hard not to be intense etc. One night about a year after we had started dating, we went out to dinner with dad and mum to a Chinese restaurant in which Rich was going to ask dad and mum "the big question". We got through our main course with a reasonable amount of conversation, but you could literally feel the tension rising during dessert. We had all ordered fried ice-cream, which is a ball of ice-cream, dipped in batter and fried in hot oil. Rich and dad both knew what was coming and they were both extremely nervous, and all they did with their ice-cream was spin it for the next 20 minutes,

before Rich finally asked dad if he could marry me, while mum and I were giggling uncontrollably. Of course dad said yes, and we were married on April 13, 1985. It was the most perfect day of my life; I felt like a fairytale princess for one very special day when almost 700 people came to see me marry my prince.

CHAPTER 2   HIGH EXPECTATIONS

All my life I knew that I would marry a pastor; I guess it was in my blood to be a pastor's wife. So when Rich and I got married, it seemed so normal for us to go into the ministry — it didn't seem bizarre or strange in the least. We were now starting a new journey, together. Not only was I leaving my home and becoming Rich's wife, but we were also leaving my home town of Townsville in Queensland and moving to another town called Maitland in New South Wales. We were also leaving the church I had known for many years, the only job I had ever known, plus all of my friends. I really had no idea at the time how many changes we, or should I say *I* was in for. I was really excited about going; little did I know how much all of these changes would affect me.

All of a sudden I had to work at fitting in; it was not automatic like I was used to. People didn't necessarily like me or understand me, or even try to be friends with me as per usual.

We went to this town because Rich had accepted the position of assistant pastor in a local church there. Everything worked out well for Rich, as it always does (he has this uncanny knack of seeing the silver lining in every cloud — sometimes I'm convinced he draws it on some of those clouds with a crayon, just so he can say he found it). But

I was really starting to struggle for the first time in my life. After we moved to Maitland, it seemed like I cried every night for about six months. I never realised how much I would miss my parents, my family, my church, and my friends. My dad had been my pastor for my whole life, and I was so naive that I really thought that all pastors were like my dad. This, as I was to discover, was not the case. Some people who are called *pastor* are very insecure individuals, and others use their office in a real political sense.

I have always had this overwhelming pull in my life to the area of music. Although I had minimal training, I had a passion for singing and playing the piano, and was very keen to learn. Coming from a large church which embraced new talent and helped people to learn, it was a real change when we moved to this quite small country church where the ethos was that only the very best musicians were accepted, and if there *was* any possibility of any talent, then you had an audition with the major musician in the church. I was asked to come to her home for an audition on the piano, after which I was told that I did not have any musical talent whatsoever! This I found to be extremely painful, but after the sting was gone I decided to prove her wrong — because I knew how wrong she was. I went back to lessons and started taking all my piano exams. My non-churched teacher was astonished that anybody could say that I had no musical talent, because even though it was raw, it was definitely there. This was one of the first examples in our new life where I had to learn that I was not as easily accepted and befriended as I had been my whole life. It was even fair to say that some people were actually threatened by my heritage. They could not just see me as *me*, but I am sure that when some people saw me they must have been looking at my whole family line, which I had now begun to see as something even *I* couldn't live up to. This would not be true of everyone; there were many people who knew us, or my parents, who were absolutely wonderful.

Things just didn't seem like they would work out for us in Maitland, as much as we both tried. We had both thought and felt from the beginning that we should have been in another town further up the road, called Singleton. We had been invited by the pastor there (Pastor Mark and Lina Cavallaro) to come and be their youth pastors, and we had wanted to go there, but got tied up in a bit of red tape and therefore ended up in Maitland. Now here we were after about ten months in Maitland, still feeling like we should have been at the other town. Thankfully circumstances turned around, and our leadership in

Maitland released us from our contract so that we could go and join the team at the Singleton church. Both pastors agreed that this was a good move for us, and so we moved up to Singleton.

The whole feel of the place was unlike Maitland and even the mind-set of the people was peculiarly different. The pastor and his wife were real goers; they were not intimidated by people. They had a brilliant attitude to the people on their team; their philosophy in general was to love the people into what they were capable of doing. One strange example of this happened not long after we moved there. The pastor asked me to be the music director for the church, which was pretty overwhelming since I was still reeling from being told I had no musical talent! But I was to learn a lesson from the Psalms — *Psalm 118:6 (NKJ) "The Lord is on my side; I will not fear. What can man do to me?"* Another important lesson I was to learn was –"Hey Girl! it is not about the talent", because my musical ability was raw talent at its best, "but the important thing is being here ready for God, and being available and faithful with what He did give, and trying to find ways to use what He gave."

Our pastors in Singleton were great role models; they had great hearts for people, they were always having people over for meals, they started the church from scratch, they were in the process of starting a Christian school, they were often counselling people, always loving people, etc, and they were always busy doing some new venture for God. It was a privilege to work with them, and we knew that they really believed in us, maybe more than I believed in us (*me*).

I would often ponder about the role models in my life — particularly my mother, and my pastor's wife — and I was sure that I could never be as good a pastor's wife as either of these great ladies. Both of them, in my mind's eye, could probably leap tall buildings blindfolded while baking a meringue at the same time, while I couldn't jump a puddle and was flat out trying to make pikelets that weren't burnt.

When I was a little girl my father used to say to me, "If you turn out to be half the woman that your mother is, then you will be a great lady". My dad's intention with that little saying was to praise mum, and tell me how brilliant she was, because he loved her and was proud of her. However, my melancholic streak caused me to read it quite differently. I would hear this — "No matter how hard you try, you will never match up to your mother." I do not in any way blame my dad, because he never intended to hurt me with that statement, and I am sure he would have been horrified had he known, but I never revealed this to him — I just learned to stuff these emotions down inside, which was later to do me a great deal of harm.

Consequently, through never dealing with this issue, I was often threatened by my mum's great abilities in ministry and life, because I thought I had to be *"her"*. I forgot the simplicity of being me. Now, this issue wasn't there every day, but every now and then it would crop up. I felt like nothing would be good enough for mum. I honestly do not think mum had any idea of what was going on inside my head, or that I was living "under her shadow".

While we were in Singleton we had our two beautiful children, Deborah and Daniel. This was a wonderful time;  they were both beautiful and healthy babies and brought incredible joy into both of our lives. While I was pregnant with our second child, Daniel, we were invited to become the senior pastors in a church in Coolum Beach, Queensland. We prayed about this and were very excited by the prospect, but could do nothing until the birth of our child. A few short months after Daniel was born we moved to Coolum Beach and started another stage in our journey of life, in more ways than we knew.

CHAPTER 3 SUPERWOMAN

From the first moments we were in Coolum Beach, Rich and I knew that everything seemed unlike anything that we had done in our previous ministry experiences. There was a large contrast for us in the change from being youth pastors and assistants to now senior ministers and running the local church. But because Rich and I are quite opposite to each other we handled the circumstances differently. Rich rose to the occasion of all the extra pressures and demands expected. Rich is one of God's awesome people who, when he gets pushed, poked, prodded or knocked out — simply bounces back with minimal fuss. It sounds silly but he reminds me of one of those bouncy inflatable toys we had as children — you push them down, and they bounce right on back.

The pressure affected me quite differently. From the very first weeks we were there I felt the same pressure to fit in and be needed and loved as I had felt in Maitland, but this time it was much stronger. Can you see how if we don't deal with those blessed little foxes, they just might come back and bite you on the bottom? This is a lesson to be learnt from Song of Solomon 2:15.

Don't get me wrong. It isn't that I didn't think we should be in Coolum, or that Rich shouldn't have taken this role as pastor — I just had no idea how all these pressures were going to affect me.

From almost the first weeks we were in Coolum one of the ways in which I didn't fit in, in my own mind, was that I had just had a baby and was a bit overweight, in a beach society where *everybody* it seemed, was blessed with a perfectly sculptured and tanned body. I can say now in hindsight that that is "simply the wrapping paper", but back then it certainly was linked to my feelings of self-worth.

I started dieting seriously within weeks of our moving to Coolum Beach, and I would walk as often as I could. I did start to lose some of the weight I had put on during pregnancy. In the most natural sense this is a normal thing for a woman to do straight after the birth of a child; to try and get back into shape; and there is absolutely nothing wrong with that, but for me there was a hint of danger which I couldn't see — I was *too* desperate to lose weight. And when you are desperate you'll do anything.

I was never obese, just a bit chubby (73kg), but my whole self - worth seemed to be entangled with the weight issue, instead of being

God's beautiful child. One illustration of this desperation was one of the diets I went on that I had read in a popular women's magazine. A well- known "doctor" advised the eating of nothing but oranges for fourteen days. This was guaranteed to help you lose three to four kilos in one week. I do not know where my common sense was! Anyhow, I didn't lose any weight at all but only ended up with a mouthful of ulcers.

I did gradually lose about ten kilos of the weight that I had put on over the next six months or so, and my focus changed to other things.

Our church was going well and there were always exciting things happening, new friends to make and people to be helped, visited and loved. I was involved with Rich as much as possible in the church; in the music team, in visiting people, and running small groups — even while our children were tiny. As they grew, my church involvement grew.

I now think that this stemmed from my obsession to be a "perfect pastor's wife", so I became "an everything to everybody" and forgot how to just be "Jo". I felt like a chameleon, because it was probably in this season that I really started to lose myself — it was almost like play acting. I was the music director, the office secretary, the district secretary, involved with the women's ministries, plus attending the play group with my son, etc. Now, I am not saying that any of those things are wrong. But in some cases I think that people can become so busy and frantic in their lives that they don't have to deal with "issues". God may just want us to rest beside still waters — but we are forcing ourselves down the white water, which may be so intense and busy that our focus is on simply surviving our own busy-ness and we don't have time for a gentle word of love or correction or to still our souls.

CHAPTER 4 AN EATING DISORDER IS BORN

It wasn't too long before that other old obsession started taunting my thought life again — "You need to be thinner, I'm sure all perfect pastors' wives are thinner than you". Our pastor - Brian Houston (Hillsong Church, Sydney) preached a message in which he mentioned "taking captive every thought". He described this as being an aggressive action, and not being kind in any way to a thought that did not line up with God's word. If I had taken captive the thoughts of "needing to be thinner, and to be perfect, and to be accepted" "Brutally Captive" at this point, I would have saved myself and my family from a tragic crisis.

Unfortunately I didn't take those thoughts captive, but I dwelt on them, and they started to become preoccupying thoughts, and this became the place where I crossed the line. I started using laxatives as a weight controlling agent in about the middle of 1990. Nobody knew about this at all, not even Rich.

I wouldn't use them all the time, but just to keep the weight at a certain level, and usually no more than twenty at a time. I would put up with intense cramping and pain, and the pain inside knowing that what I was doing to my body had to be harmful. I knew it was wrong, but I would do it anyway — but not joyfully, not that that makes it any better. I think if you dwell on anything long enough, you will do it even if you don't want to. A lot of it comes down to what you focus on. If you keep on thinking about something and looking at it long enough, you will probably go there.

I think that there are seasons when we are allowed to believe that everything is "cool" or "in control", and this was the season I experienced for at least another eighteen months — where things rocked on as normal, except for the issue of the laxatives that I knew I should deal with but would not. This is called "grace". I believe God was giving me every chance to sort through these issues.

We were able to build our first home, which was another shift of focus for me. There were the months of planning, choosing colours, laminates, carpets, tap fittings, etc. This was an enjoyable time for me, purely because it had no pressure attached, except it should be a "perfect house". The whole planning stage was exciting for me, and hard work for both of us. As we were owner builders of our little house, and there were a lot of the labouring jobs which we did ourselves. Rich oversaw the building project, which he did splendidly.

Within a few short months our lives were very different. We had never owned our own home before, having lived in approximately six rental homes before this, and now finally we had our own home.

I am sure that sometimes things are purely meant to be a blessing to us — like our beautiful little house was. But deep down inside of me I didn't think I deserved it, so I started from the moment we moved in to become far more obsessed than before. My focus was on two things now — having a spotless house, and getting thinner (although by this point I *was* thinner at approx 58kgs).

I started walking a lot more, and eating a lot less, and keeping a perfect house, and being a perfect pastor's wife — which is way too weird for a mother of two little children. Deborah was now in grade one and Daniel was in day care. This should have been the most enjoyable time of my life — but I missed it. It seems like I became a bird in a cage.

I started to lose more weight, and at first the comments I would receive were great — "Boy you're looking great Jo. Have you lost weight?", and because I had lost focus, it didn't take long at all until the comments were — "You have lost too much weight. What is wrong with you? Don't you know you will die?" The effect that these last comments had on me was introversion and I began to hide in my shell more and more.

I still loved my God, but He wasn't God of my whole heart as He once was. I still had good times with family, friends and in our church environment. I still knew God's voice when He would speak to me. He is so patient with us — even when we are His runaway sheep.

CHAPTER 5   HONESTY OF SORTS

Rich and I were invited to go to Brisbane for a weekend marriage seminar to train to be facilitators of the course in our own church and region. God was really smiling about this one — it is almost hilarious how He can get you involved in something on behalf of other people, but in reality it is because He wants to work on your life. If I had known that this weekend would be focusing on us, I would not have gone.

However we did go, because we genuinely had hearts to help other people.

This was a fairly intense course of lectures, homework, honesty, and opening up to one another. At first I thought I could just smile my way through it and nothing would change. But there came a point on the second day when we were asked to go home and be completely transparent with our partners about any hidden issues, share them honestly and openly, and forgive each other lovingly in the privacy of our own room. I knew I could no longer keep Rich at arms-length regarding the laxative abuse, which had by now been going on for several years, so I plucked up all my courage and told him about it. It seemed like the hardest thing I had ever had to do up to that point. Rich was great, but I don't really think he understood the ramifications of the whole thing, and the power that it held over me. He could see that I was really affected by it and was very loving towards me.

The next day people were given the opportunity to share any breakthroughs they had had the previous night. Although this was the last thing I wanted to do, one of the leaders encouraged me to share, and deep down I knew that I should. So I went up before the group and shared about the laxative abuse, my decline in eating (as I was now down to about 51 kgs), the isolation that I was starting to feel, and the effect I must have been having on my two little children. I told them how my little boy had said to me, "Mummy, you will die if you don't eat!" I felt extremely vulnerable because I had been covering up for so long, and up to this point I had not even named my problem.

As the chapter indicates, this was an honesty of sorts, because I could not be honest with my parents, my family or those in our church. I would not allow Rich to tell anyone what was really going on. In fact, if my parents rang us up (as they had not seen us for quite a while), I didn't even want to speak to them as I could not face them. Because *I* was the one who was supposed to hold the whole family together, now I felt that I had let them down badly.

At the time we both counted this as a victory of sorts, but in actual fact it was part of a chain of events that opened up a Pandora's Box.

CHAPTER 6   PANDORA'S BOX OPENED

It wasn't too long after this that several of the churches in the region hosted large rallies with a guest speaker from Melbourne. I went along to as many meetings as possible. They were great meetings where many people committed their hearts to God, were baptised in water, and filled with the Holy Spirit as described in the book of Acts in the Bible.

It was a thrill for me to be in these meetings, where there was so much life. Fasting and prayer was promoted during the build-up to each set of meetings and I got caught up with this and began fasting. At first my motives were great — for God to bless the meetings, for people to be delivered from their bondages, and for people with sicknesses to be healed. But I soon learned that fasting was another quick weight loss mechanism.

So I would do extended fasts with mixed motives. My husband was not in favour of this fasting at all, but I was quite rebellious and persisted with it. I began to lose a lot more weight (down to approx 46 kgs), but still I was persisting. I don't know how I thought I could ever be of help to anyone else; when I was in such desperate need of help myself.

One thing I have now learned is that you will generally be tempted on the level of your weakness, and mine was a weight loss weakness. How easy it was for the tempter to bring along the fasting issue at the very point when I would spiritualise it. It is just as well that God can see our hearts, because we can actually deceive our own hearts and fool ourselves as to why we do certain things.

I really had myself believing at that point that I was right in God's eyes in what I was doing. If only I had lined up my beliefs with God's word, things would have been different.

My fasts at this stage would go for around ten to thirteen days at a time — long enough to lose hunger and all interest in food.

The thing about fasting is that it opens you up to spiritual realms. I believe that if your heart is clean and pure before God then this is a great tool to use in moderation because God can bring clarity and revelation to your heart. But if there are issues that you refuse to deal with, or if you are in disobedience to God when you go into fasting, you may become a target for attack — as you are exposing your weakness.

CHAPTER 7   GOD - I'LL GIVE YOU ANYTHING - BUT NOT MY WEIGHT ISSUES

One of the main characteristics of an eating disorder, more than the food issue, is CONTROL. Everything else in your life can be like a whirlpool spinning out of control, but at least you have control over your weight (or it has control over you). The hardest thing for a person with an eating disorder to do is to allow someone else to be in charge of their weight, because it is like giving up. Because everything else in your life is such a nightmare, the one area that is in control is your weight — at least the part about not putting it on.

I would view anyone who tried to tell me about food or putting on weight to be overbearing and controlling.

I always had this strong belief that, whenever we would talk with people who had problems, even if I could see what a person's problem was, I had no right to delve into it unless they opened the subject and gave me a door of opportunity. I still try to hold to this policy today.

Weirdly enough, when I was in the midst of my problems other people did not have the same philosophy. There were numerous people who would give unsolicited advice and opinions and even reprimands. These did not help at all, but made me pull back from these people, as I felt that they were attacking me and did not care about me or love me. One lady felt it was her obligation to ring around all the ladies in the church and advise them about "Jo's eating disorder". I cannot express what utter disgust I felt when I learned about this, because she did not learn this from us, but heard about it on the grapevine, and did not have the decency to talk to us about it (not that we would have been open with her).

On the other hand there were some people in our lives who loved us beyond loving, and cared beyond caring, and because of this we were able to be open with them. Kieran and Janet McKean were such a couple, and were a lifeline to us both. We were in a position where we were supposed to be helping people, but at this point of our lives Kieran and Janet were helping us.

I don't regard that I had given this problem over to God — I would give it to Him and take it back within five minutes. I did constantly pray and talk to God about it, but very rarely listened to God about it.

One day I was on one of my rigorous walks and I was talking to God *'about it'* and I remember praying these words — *"God you can have anything else in my life - but you cannot have my weight problem!"* How stupid. That was inviting trouble into my life, but it was also an issue of trust. I could not trust anyone else to be in charge of my problem, when in actual fact I was making a bigger mess of it than if I had handed it to my Creator.

I don't know why I couldn't trust God, who held the universe in His hands, to be able to sort out my problem, or why I thought I could do a better job of handling it than Him. That little statement I had made opened the way for disaster and, believe me, disaster came.

Dear Diary

July 1

I haven't eaten anything more than a couple of low fat carobs for days. I am so tired all the time. Today all I did was take Daniel to pre-school and then sleep.

CHAPTER 8   THE BORDER OF DISORDER

From this time on there was no more fooling around — I just simply was not in control anymore. You may have heard the saying, "on the border of disorder". Well I had crossed over the line, and now the disorder was controlling me. From this point on; even when I wanted to come back over that line into being well, I simply could not do that; it was a long hard battle. People may think that a person with anorexia should just eat, and then they would get well. But a person who is in the grip of an obsession like this will know that it is not as simple as just eating and getting fatter. It can be very complex.

I had already been enduring long fasts of ten to thirteen days as previously mentioned, but that now escalated into months without eating anything substantial, possibly only a rice cake in a twenty-four hour period. The results of this were devastating.

I could no longer exercise (to lose weight) because I had no energy (from losing weight). There was also no energy to even be rational or logical. Many days I would walk my son down to the pre-school, walk home and sleep the rest of the day. I entered a long period where I was numb, without feelings or emotions, just numb. This was similar to the story I had heard of an African mother who had just had her children slain through war, and walked many miles to a refugee camp — she was not distraught with grief because her body was too starved to experience emotion.

I still played the piano every Sunday for church, though several times I was at the point of fainting. There were just some things I couldn't let go of, and playing was one of them. I was using it as something to hide behind. It also kept me busy so other thoughts did not crowd me. But I must have looked ridiculous — a stick woman playing the keys.

One thing I would hate was those interminable potluck cell dinners. There was so much food! I was even afraid to look at it, but somehow I would manage to get through by eating very little, or just stirring my food around on the plate several times, pushing it on and off my fork to give the illusion of having eaten something! The deception was the core of this whole thing — the whole name of the game was to fool people and lose weight by improper means, the whole time pretending that it was okay because I am naturally thin.

One of those potluck dinners which I couldn't get out of, and couldn't get out of eating either, led me to the other side of the eating disorder — purging through vomiting. This became my enemy/friend, because although it would help me get rid of those calories, it was also as if I was losing any last bit of self-respect I had left. Self-hatred really took hold of me from this point. This became a daily ritual— whatever little I did eat would be purged one way or another. My body was losing electrolytes alarmingly.

Dear Diary

July 20

Cell group dinner tonight. I hate the fear that I feel in all my pretence. I am so frightened that I will be caught out and my secret will be out. This again makes me feel a freak, as I know I am not normal.

CHAPTER 9 THE PROBLEM GETS A NAME - MISS ANNA REXIA TO THE STAND PLEASE

One day at Janet's house, I came to the realization and understanding that I needed medical help. Up to this point I would not hear of getting help, because I was denying the enormity of the issue. Janet and I talked this through and I agreed to see my local GP who hadn't seen me for approx fourteen months. When I went for the appointment she knew immediately that I was sick with something to be that thin (now approx 47kgs). But I had to come forward and tell her what was wrong, about my problem with eating, or lack of it, and actually verbalize that I thought I might have ANOREXIA! She was very professional in her quick actions to get me in to see a psychiatrist in a nearby town, and these appointments were to start in approx six weeks. In the meantime I was to continue seeing Dr Joanna every week.

The very first threat of hospitalisation came up with Dr Joanna. During one of the appointments she said to me in no uncertain terms that she had the legal right to place me in hospital to be force-fed against my will if I refused to eat. She was under a legal obligation not to allow me to die. Obviously she saw my position from a different angle than I did. But somehow, thankfully, I just scraped through without being hospitalised.

I started psychotherapy in August 1993 with Dr Lynda, who was a broad-field psychiatrist, whom I didn't think had much experience in the field of eating disorders, outside of the teenage range.

However it was definitely confirmed that I did have anorexia nervosa, and treatment was commenced. She had horrible methods. I had to weigh in at each appointment, and she also told Rich that he had to follow me around and stop me from vomiting and using laxatives. In other words she wanted to turn him into my jailer, which he had never been. I must add that Rich was put in a very awkward position — which he did not like or enjoy.

I began to feel very hemmed in and I needed someone to rescue me from the mess I had placed myself in, and increasingly felt the need for my dad to come and blot it all out and make it all better. But my dad couldn't make any of it better, because I had isolated myself from my family and they had no idea of the crisis I was in.

Dad and mum were on a holiday for three months for their long service leave, and were currently in London. I missed them so much — but the walls I had built around myself shut me in.

After thinking very hard about my situation I decided to take the plunge and rang dad & mum, I was very nervous but I felt I had nothing left to lose — I had already let them down. But they needed to know, and I needed their support.

Dad answered the phone and said "Hi Honey, what's wrong?", and my reply was "I have anorexia", which completely stunned him. They had not seen me for a long time or even spoken to me for a good while, and it must have seemed like that comment came out of the blue. He said "Who told you that rubbish?", and I said "My psychiatrist". I am sure that both of them felt like the air was taken out of their balloon. I know they must have felt desolate being on the other side of the world, and there was nothing they could do about the situation. But they did know how to pray, and pray they did. They also decided that mum would come up from Sydney for a couple of weeks when they got back from their trip. I was so cynical at the time that I thought, how the heck does mum think she is going to fix this in four weeks when it's been going on for years, and I was extremely nervous about her coming up.

Dr Lynda was making enquiries about getting me admitted into Prince Charles Hospital in Brisbane around the time that mum was due to come. The doctors were very concerned about my health and wanted to get my weight up (currently 46.5 kg), but she decided to put that on hold due to my mother coming to visit.

Mum arrived on November 2 and I went down to the Maroochydore airport to pick her up. She was planning to stay for a month. I was so apprehensive that I had starved for four days before she came and my weight was now down to 45 kgs.

Mum's first comment was "Well, you are not as thin as I was expecting!", which got me mad. I had rather wanted her to be shocked. In hindsight it was probably the over-sized jumper I was wearing to hide my bones.

We had some good breakthroughs in that we were able to have some in-depth talks about issues. During one of these discussions I told mum about the years of laxative abuse, which absolutely floored her. During another talk we had, I told her that I couldn't remember her holding me, cuddling me or being affectionate with me as a child, which led me to believe that she did not love me and that I wasn't planned or wanted. Mum denied this to be the case, and explained how I was very much loved. What I now understand is that a whole lot comes down to your perception. Something may be true, but if a person perceives it differently, then their truth is coloured by that.

After one of our long talks, I went to my room and read the bible and this verse jumped out at me — *Psalm 118: 17-18 (NIV) "I will not die but live, and will proclaim what the Lord has done. The Lord has chastened me severely, but He has not given me over to death."*

This verse was another lifeline for me to hold onto, because I knew that God did not want me to die. Although I was blurry in my mind, I knew there was some sort of threat, even though it seemed unreal — it was kind of like being in a daze. Everybody else seemed aware of the enormity of the problem, and half of the time I really could see what they were so upset and panicky about, but the other half I thought they were acting way over the top.

While mum was visiting us our State Assemblies of God Pastor's Conference was scheduled and Rich was going. I also wanted to go, so mum and I just went down for one day during the conference. Mum wanted some of the leaders to pray with me privately, and although my mind was screaming against this, I consented. Both Pastor John Lewis and Pastor Chris Petersen were obviously moved by my situation and they were both loving and supportive. While they prayed, Pastor Lewis shared with me that *"Jesus is my judge and He touches my chin to lift it to Him, I can't lift my head only He can."* He also shared the verse in Psalms which became a revelation to me — *"My glory and the lifter of my head."*

Mum wanted me to eat normally with the family, which was something I had not done for eons. So I tried, just to please her, but it wasn't long before I was panicking and sneaking off to vomit or to use laxatives. I am sure she was horrified by all of this and didn't know what to do, because one thing is for sure, you can't *control* an anorexia patient. It seemed like she thought if she came and lived with us and fed me and showed me she loved me for a while, it would be better. But as I know now, anorexia is based on a lie. You lose weight by not being truthful. You begin lying about how much you did eat, when you didn't eat at all. The "lie of anorexia" is so insidious — it says "*You are not beautiful and accepted as you are. You are different. You are a freak.*" When you are as thin as paper anorexia says *"you are fat"*. The lies are thorns in your mind and it would take a miracle to unscramble my mind. She must have felt as helpless as Rich, not knowing what to do at all.

Dear Diary

August 11

I visited the psychiatrist with Rich today. She insisted that Rich has to now be involved in my treatment as things have become so serious. She was very straight with me. She said I have to get better from this illness or I will die. She insisted that Rich has to take on the responsibility to stop me from vomiting and that he will have to now be my minder. This terrifies me — this will tear us apart.

August 26

God showed me today that because Rich and I are one flesh not two flesh, and because I am his and he is mine, I have no right to do anything to my body (which is Rich's body) that he doesn't agree with.

August 28

On Friday night we were at the McKean's and I was looking through some of Janet's Vogue magazines to make sure that I looked as thin as the models – but God, you know that I actually looked heaps skinnier than they did – they actually looked healthier than me.

September 2

We went down to Brisbane today to visit Richie's family. His mum confronted me again – she held my face and said "you are going to die". I cried, and Rich intervened and protected me.

September 7

I rang Richie's mum and talked to her. I said "Mum, I am not anorexic but I have been under so much pressure this year with so many hurts. I also told Mum Luhrs that I am having therapy, and that I have been adhering to strict diets. She turned right around and became my defender instead of my accuser. (While I was this ill my thoughts were irrational and illogical — Mum Luhrs was never my accuser, but that is how I would perceive anyone who made comments about my weight.) I am sorry God I couldn't be completely honest with Rich's mum, but it was a breakthrough. Rich told me afterwards that he was so proud of me.

CHAPTER 10   SICKNESS IN THE TREE

That night I opened up to mum about the way I felt about the situation regarding my grandfather. Mum's dad was a minister, who I perceived to have had little time for any of his children (once they were grown up), and less for his grandchildren. Many years ago before I was born, his wife (my grandmother) died of cancer, and within a few years he married a spinster. From this time on he spent less and less time with his natural family, and more and more with the surrogate family he and his wife created from the people who surrounded them. These people became virtual family to my grandfather and step-grandmother, and they called them father and mother. So we his *"real"* family had limited access to him, as my step-grandmother had no link to us, and promoted the other virtual family in their lives.

One day many years ago we went to visit grandad, after a holiday we had had. Three of us kids raced up to the door and knocked, and were answered by a lady we didn't know. She asked if she could help us, and we said, "We are here to see our Grandad", and she called out, "Father, you have some visitors". This was the strangest experience. It is good to know that when I want to talk to my heavenly dad, I don't have to get some stranger's permission! Anyway, we were ushered into the lounge room for afternoon tea, and after a few polite words they started asking my dad tricky spiritual questions about what God was saying in the church today. All I remember feeling was shock as we three children tried to show them our holiday photos, and they didn't give a rip, so we went outside. Mum tried to point out to them how we children just wanted them to be interested in us, and couldn't they spare us a few moments? My step-grandmother pointed out that since we hadn't been invited to come to their home we probably shouldn't be talking like that. At this point we all left, and didn't see grandad again for many years.

I have felt contempt for people who "do God's work, but reject God's precious gift of family", but I also struggled with a great amount of rejection. I would often ponder, "*What is wrong with me, that Grandad couldn't love me?*" When I was a tiny child and he visited, he would call me his little princess, but I am positive that princesses get a better deal than that.

I actually went to a large family reunion about six months after my mother's visit to me in Coolum, and I was at the party for over two ½ hours before my grandfather actually even knew who I was. He proceeded to invite us to come up and see the great ministry set-up they had built for God, but I was not interested in seeing any ministry they had built for God, because they were not even interested in their own grandchildren. I was simply past trying to please him, and I thought the whole thing was hypocrisy. I also did not have any grace added to my life due to my experience.

On the other side of my family (my dad's parents), there were also major complications.

My gramps (grandfather) was an independent minister of his own small congregation. One day when my dad was sixteen years of age, dad went to an Assemblies of God church in the town and re-committed his life to God. He came home to tell his folks about it, thinking that they would be as excited as he was. This was not the case. My gramp's response was, "You will either never go to that church again, or you will leave this house". So dad was asked to leave the family home at the tender age of sixteen years for going to a different church; not for being a drunkard, or immoral, or on drugs. I thought that this was more of that same hypocrisy.

Consequently, dad was separated from his parents for twenty years. As we were growing up we didn't know anything about dad's parents at all.

However, when my little brother was born, miraculously the family was restored and we were all invited to go over to Perth to have Christmas together. I was twelve the first time I met my gramps and nanny and my four aunties. We had a wonderful time there with all of them, but it what stood out more for me was, "*Why didn't you all want to know us before?*"

This side of the family has now been beautifully restored, but my wish (as I'm sure was God's wish), was that none of it should have happened in the first place — it was senseless and stupid to forsake flesh and blood over a "nothing".

I have learned first-hand that family must come before ministry, simply because if you can't minister and relate to your family, who can you minister to?

Mum and I talked over all of these issues, and I told her of the real rejection I had felt, especially from my grandfather. I couldn't understand why he couldn't love us. I kept going back over the same ground — what was wrong with us that he couldn't love us?

Although this chapter may surprise some at what sadness and dysfunction can exist within a Christian home, God's grace still covers all. I want to end this chapter off with a wonderful story of His faithfulness.

In the last year after my step-grandmother passed away, my grandfather (Herbert Westbrook) was amazingly restored to all of his children, and God took away the years of separation that the locusts had eaten. I know that even with my own mother this restoration meant so much to her, and there was incredible healing. Grandfather went on to be with Jesus earlier this year, and I thank Jesus for his grace in giving my family this one beautiful year to take away from all that had been.

Dear Diary

November 9 (45.6 kilos)

I consumed today

225 calories – Porridge, 2 dates, 1 cup Sustagen

40 calories – 2 coffees

65 calories –1 cup low fat soup and coffee

95 calories – Caro, 1 piece of low fat date cake

240 calories – Stir fry chicken and rice

130 calories – Apple crumble and low fat custard

15 calories – Caro

Total – 810 GOOD GIRL JO

(These written accounts of daily food intakes were religious, and the comment at the end would be either – Good Girl Jo or Bad Girl Jo, you have to try harder to keep the calories down.)

November 2

Mum arrived tonight. I have been so apprehensive about this that I have starved for four days, I have just been so nervous of her visit. I went to the doctor yesterday and she had made inquiries at the Prince Charles Hospital in Brisbane about me being admitted for 3-4 weeks to feed me up to 46 kilos — she thought it was the only way. When Mum arrived today my weight was 45 kilos. I was afraid of mum being bossy and controlling – but instead she was very gentle. After we put the children to bed, we had tears together in the kitchen, when she said she loved me. I believed her.

CHAPTER 11   THE NIGHT FROM HELL

At the start of mum's visit things seemed fine on the surface, but there came a point when everything went back to the huge struggle I had been in before, except more hidden. Instead of just plain starving, I *had* to eat because I was expected to, but the vomiting started again and the laxative abuse as well.

One night, I'm not really sure how it started; I locked myself in our bedroom and wouldn't let anyone in. I must have been in there for several hours. Mum was getting frantic, knocking on the door and calling for me to let her in. I was huddled up in a ball on the bed for the longest time, my brain was pounding and I didn't want to let her in. I remember physically shaking, and although I don't remember what I was afraid of, I know I was afraid, very afraid.

After a long while I went into the walk-in robe and huddled in a ball in the corner and hid. I am not sure what I was hiding from, but I felt like I was totally losing my mind. My grip on any kind of reality was going — it was like swimming in molasses. I know now that it was freaking mum out, especially not really knowing what was happening, but there was nothing she could do as I had locked her out earlier, and Rich was not home.

For a long time I just huddled in the corner of the robe, rocking and shaking and crying.

Eventually Rich came home, and he says it was like he walked into a bombshell. Mum filled him in on the fact that I had locked her out and something was wrong, so he had to break into the bedroom and see what was happening. Rich says that even before they opened the door he sensed death present and he was terrified that they would open the door and find me dead on the floor.

He jemmied the door open, and could not find me. Initially he thought I had escaped out of the window and ran away, but he kept looking and found me huddled in the back of the walk-in robe, shaking. He told mum to stay out, because he could see how fragile I was. He got me out of the robe, and rocked me and stroked my hair until I fell asleep.

The nightmare seemed to subside by morning, but we all knew this thing was no game, and had to be handled carefully. There was one other mad episode that happened a few weeks later, when, late one night, I don't know how I got there, but Rich found me outside walking in the rain in my pyjamas. My mind was extremely fragile — sometimes I was so numb that I didn't know what I was doing.

Mum decided to cut short her stay and head for home. I think she came to the realisation that the problem was not going to go away overnight, and that her best efforts would be from home on her knees.

Dear Diary

September 8

Rich and I talked for hours tonight, all the way until midnight. Rich told me that if I had to go to hospital or if I stopped eating again he only had two options: 1. Resign from the church 2. Tell the congregation my problem.

I died inside. I felt like my safety net had been smashed. Over the last few days the pressure had been so great that I felt it would be safer to cut down my food intake so I could not gain weight, and maybe I would be safer in hospital. But now this option was removed. Now I could not afford to get any worse, as it would kill me for everyone to know what was going on (I honestly had no concept that they couldn't already see what was going on). Now I have to keep eating so I at least stay my current weight.

I rang Janet tonight because I was so distressed — praise God for good friends. Janet told me to spend some time speaking in tongues to build myself up in God. This I did and it was a great help.

November 4 (45 kilos)

Today I realised while I was praying to you, God, that I was actually deceived because I had been deceiving others. I had been lying about my illness by hiding it. Those who deceive are deceived.

After this I started looking through the Bible for scriptures on life and health — you showed me one scripture that will pull me through.

Psalm 118:7 "I will not die but live and will proclaim what the Lord has done. The Lord has chastened me severely, but He has not given me over to death". All I could see as I was reading this was the vision I had seen of myself laying on the bathroom floor with all the blood coming from my slit wrists. Thank you God for giving me your promise of life.

You also showed me Proverbs 3:7-8 "Do not be wise in your own eyes: fear the Lord and shun evil. This will bring health to your body and nourishment to your bones."

Lord you are showing me that I can only trust your own wisdom, my own brings me undone.

CHAPTER 12   HELP ME IF YOU CAN I'M FEELING DOWN

It was a little while after this that we spent some time with some friends of ours from Brisbane (Mark and Lina) who were holidaying at Noosa. These friends were actually our former pastors from Singleton who had since moved to Brisbane and pioneered a church there. During the course of our time with them, I shared with Lina what was happening. I felt safe with Lina and I knew she would never condemn me.

Mark and Lina were connected in Brisbane with an awesome doctor whom they were sure could be a great help to me. We agreed for them to set up an appointment and we would go down and see her.

From the moment we walked into Dr Carolyn Russell's office I knew I was in safe hands. She spent over two and ½ hours, listening to our story, discussing all the options, and working through the gravity of the situation.

As far as she was concerned there was really no option but to resign from the church, move to another location and get proper professional help. Even though I was already under a psychiatrist, she was a broadly trained professional, and did not have a lot of skill with my problem. Dr Russell felt it imperative that I see a psychiatrist who specialises in eating disorders, of whom she could recommend three in Brisbane. Dr Russell immediately wrote a letter for us to give to our church board which stated that in her medical opinion there was no other recourse but for Rich and myself to resign our positions because of my health issues.

So Rich and I had a lot of talking to do, — but in the end there was little choice, we knew what we had to do. We knew if we stayed I would get weaker and die, because by now everything was so stressful, and my ministry role was now "too hard", probably because it wasn't flowing out of "who I was", but "who I was pretending to be".

Firstly we had a board meeting to let the elders know of our decision to resign. Initially they were stunned, but as we talked them through, they could see we were not negotiable on our decision, and they were therefore very supportive. As I was still freaking out about everybody knowing what was wrong with me, they were all in agreement that when the announcement was made there was to be no mention of exactly what was wrong, simply that for health reasons and to get professional health care we would be moving to Brisbane. This was announced to the church, in early December, and then we packed up and moved to Brisbane at the end of January 1994.

This was probably the hardest thing Rich ever had to do in his entire life — it really broke his heart because he loved pastoring and was excellent at it. But he knew he would lose me if we didn't leave. I honour him now, because I know what he did for me — he laid down his life and desires so that I would have a chance to live. I know that most couples never have to experience anything this grave, but in my case I have the experience of knowing that my husband "walked across broken glass" for me. Even though I couldn't appreciate his sacrifice for me then (because I was so irrational), I do now. If you are reading this Rich, *"I love you babe! Thank you for giving me a chance to live"*.

We had a lot of changes initially — settling our two children into a new school, finding a house, trying to sell our house in Coolum, while Rich did another year of Bible College while working part-time in the cleaning industry.

I went to see Dr Russell every week during the waiting period while she was trying to get me in to see the specialist psychiatrist.

Now that the children were settled in school, and Rich's work and studies had started, loneliness settled further on me, and I would hide for hours every day under the quilt covers on my bed. I lost more weight and hit an all time low of 41 kgs — I had previously been advised by Dr Lynda that if I went under 45 kgs, with all the laxative abuse, I could die at any time because my heart could stop due to the electrolyte imbalances. Because eating disorders are extremely complex, in my particular case my body would not physically have tolerated any more weight loss, unlike some of the high profile cases where some patients' weight decreased to 25kgs. In my case, because of the laxative abuse and the vomiting, I was facing a possible heart failure. This was a very real threat, as there were many times when I could feel my heart physically changing its rhythms, or stopping and then starting, and then speeding up. This is the same threat that took Karen Carpenter's life.

Eventually I started treatment with my new psychiatrist, Dr Malcolm Foxcroft, whom I was to see weekly for the next fifteen months. He got me straight onto a course of Prozac anti-depressant tablets to lift my depression to a manageable level.

For weeks, I sat in the chair in his office like a stunned mullet, hardly saying a thing, because initially I didn't even know if I could trust him, and I didn't know what methods he would use on me. Was he going to be like Dr Lynda or not? He really had to draw everything out of me, as there was no emotion any more. I actually did not care if I lived or died — it was irrelevant.

But slowly, as the weeks went on, I came to trust Malcolm, and came to know that he was on my side. He was not out to hurt me. His approach was very different to that of my other doctor. Because this was his speciality he knew how to treat the patients with the best methods to bring the desired results. I don't mean to criticize my first psychiatrist, but her methods with me were not effective.

Little by little, Dr Malcolm brought me physically back from death row. He would teach me how to eat, breaking down the strict rules of food, and bad food lists I had recorded in my brain. He helped me to feel safe about food, and would give me homework for each week. Never once did I feel he tried to control me, which was extremely important, because he knew and I knew that it would backfire if he did. Instead, he worked *with* me and not against me. In fact, he never once weighed me, unlike Dr Lynda who had previously forced me to weigh in every week. Instead, he would use his own intelligence to see whether I was gaining or losing — remember, he was a specialist and was extremely hard to fool.

When my weight was more manageable (50 kgs), we started to deal with all of the other issues one by one. I actually learned so much about myself through this counselling. At first it was overwhelming because I had not had any emotional feelings for so long, but now that I was a bit healthier physically, all of these emotions came back, but on a stronger scale. There were days when I was incredibly angry, and yet I had always perceived that anger was bad. I didn't even know how to be angry, and my tendencies were to stuff the anger back down inside again. But he would teach me to express it without being harmful. I remember one day standing in my kitchen, feeling all of these emotions and not knowing what to do with them, and eventually picking up a dinner plate and dropping it on the kitchen floor. I did feel foolish, but at least I was expressing the feeling instead of allowing it to eat me up. All of the hurts that I had previously pushed down, in my life surfaced one by one, and we had to work through them.

We talked a lot about my issues with the church, and being in a minister's family, my grandparents, etc. There were times during my counselling sessions when my emotions were going full force — I would be so confused that I wanted to walk away completely from my Christian heritage. Dr Malcolm, even though he himself was not a

Christian, would never allow me to do this — he was teaching me to face my problems and not run away. The typical "anorexic" response is to put your head in the sand and ignore the issue, and he would teach me not to do that. In hindsight, I thank God for sending me to Dr Malcolm because he could have easily coloured my view on Christianity, but he did not.

Dr Malcolm was a brilliant doctor and did me a great service, but he told me in no uncertain terms, "Jo, I can't cure your anorexia. You are going to have it all of your life, and even if you ever get over it there is a 50 per cent chance of your becoming a bulimic. I can teach you how to manage your illness, somewhat like a recovered alcoholic, and I can teach you the steps you will need to take to keep in under control."

So at this stage we were working on keeping it managed, because there wasn't much hope of ever living without it. I am sure you can understand this — a person can put the weight back on necessary to survive, but still have the illness ravaging their soul.

Dear Diary

February 3

I went shopping today – I am so frustrated I can't buy underwear that fits; I can't buy bras small enough. My whole life it was always the opposite.

CHAPTER 13   ISOLATION SEPARATED ME FROM THE ONES I LOVED

One of the repercussions of this type of sickness is the way it separates you from everyone around you. The insidious way it would work was initially you were losing weight to gain acceptance from those people who were around you, but you ended up separated from them because you could not relate to them, and they could not relate to you, and their acceptance was no longer relevant.

Initially I wanted to be thin to please Rich, although he never expected this or asked for it, but slowly and surely I ended up with a body that could not please Rich. My own mother's description of what I looked like when she came to stay, and helped me bathe, was that I looked like a holocaust victim.

I used to think it would be great when I lost some weight; I could join in and go to the beach and have fun with the family — but the end result for me was that my family became so dysfunctional, (Rich, Deb and Dan), and then there was me totally separated from them.

We didn't eat together; we didn't play together; there were very few things we could do together. It wasn't that I didn't want to join in — I did want to, but I couldn't. My own walls separated me from them; as did my walls separate me from my extended family and friends.

I also had developed the false idea that everybody was against me, and out to hurt and attack me. At times I felt like I had people all around me who were waiting for me to fail, and failing was what I was doing pretty well. Some days were better than others, but on one of the bad days I remember sensing that people who were around me had great big machetes ready to slice me up into a million pieces and discard me.

This is another of the lessons I have learned — don't trust your feelings alone, because feelings are incredibly fickle. I was dying of starvation, and yet I felt fat — what irony.

One of the sayings I have learned at Hillsong Church is, "Don't bring your beliefs down to the level of your experience, but bring your experience up to the level of your beliefs". This is what I mean by not trusting your feelings, because they can get you tangled up so fast you'll end up looking like spaghetti in knots

CHAPTER 14   SUICIDE WAS CALLING MY NAME

Anorexia nervosa is a disease that has a huge focus on death (physically, mentally and relationally). It is literally a thief of life and hope to any family who encounter it. So there should be no great surprise that I experienced times of being quite suicidal.

The first experience I had of this nature happened to me when we were still in Coolum. I had this recurring dream — every time I shut my eyes I would see myself on the bathroom floor covered in blood, holding a large kitchen knife. I was afraid to shut my eyes because of this dream, but then sometimes I would even see it in the daytime. I actually had no desire to end my life in this way, but I know that the "enemy of my soul" desperately wanted my life to end, as he was throwing his best ammunition my way.

I ended up sharing this dream with a pastor's wife colleague of mine, and she told me that she had seen me in the same dream and had been praying for me. Thankfully this subsided.

After we moved to Brisbane, I experienced great loneliness, because every part of our environment was new — new house, new school, new work, and new doctor. There was nothing familiar except for one or two people I knew. Before and during my first months of counselling with Dr Malcolm, I would become overshadowed by a real feeling of wanting to die, and a willingness to end my life.

I would spend time plotting ways of overdosing, because I genuinely believed that I had become such a burden to those around me, that they would truly be far better off without me.

I remember thinking that it would be better for me to die so that Rich could have the chance to find a better wife — one who would not put him through so much pain — and the kids, well, what would they need me for? They would all truly be better off without me.

But thank God I never did anything to act on those schemes from "Hell's PA system". Satan is such a liar, and he so wants to take out good people who can be effective in helping others, that he will prey on your weaknesses and vulnerabilities if you allow him. Don't let him rip you off — you are God's beautiful creation, chosen to be a vessel to help others.

Once again that scripture from Psalm 118 came to me — *"I will not die but live and will proclaim what the Lord has done."* Here is another choice example of bringing our feelings up to the level of God's Word.

CHAPTER 15   I CAN'T EVEN SING ANYMORE

I have always loved singing, even as a child. I always had an affinity with music. I remember one of the most exciting gifts I received as a child was one of those miniature grand pianos, about 40cm wide, and it was white with a lift up lid. he reason why I loved it was because it was a gift that touched my soul. I definitely do not claim to be a professional or brilliant musician or singer, but just a child of God who loves his sounds.

So as I became ill, I still persisted in playing the piano every week. But instead of the enjoyment it had always been, and instead of it being easy as it had always been, it became an escape mechanism, and the words I was singing, I was singing blindly — you could not call it worship, just hollow singing. This continued until we left Coolum.

When we left Coolum and moved to Brisbane, we decided to go to Northside Christian Family, which was a reasonably large church. Rich and I felt the need to be in a church where people didn't know us too much, and we could hide in the crowd to recover.

They had a good music team there, compared to what we were used to in our smaller church, and we were glad, but the one thing I noticed as my counselling progressed — the song in my soul was dead.

We would faithfully go along to church, but I couldn't even sing. There was no desire or energy to do so. As I was to learn, God was dealing with me over honesty, right to the very core of my soul. Because this disease is full of lies, I had to go through this process about the "honesty issue".

As time went on, and I gradually came to sing a little at a time, but if a they were singing a line like "*Lord I give you my heart, I give you my soul, have your way in me*", or something similar that required a consecrated heart to God, and I knew that I would be going home to be obsessing about weight issues or vomiting, then I knew before God I could not sing that song, and I also knew that God was understanding of this, because I was relearning honesty.

As I came to flourish, the whole singing part of my life came into a new dimension with God that I never even knew before. I understand now that worship is not a song I sing in one moment before God, but it is the life I live before God, and out of that the song is born. It is the reason I was born, to worship Jesus in my everyday actions, and relations and also with my voice. What I am in my private world will come across in my public world. If I am worshipping God publicly and my private life is telling God a different story, which should He listen to? I was learning the hard way that God wanted my heart and not my song only, but when I gave Him my heart, He then would give me my song.

CHAPTER 16 ONE STEP FORWARDS AND TWO STEPS BACK

There were so many times in my counselling when I could see a glimpse of progress, but it wasn't long before I felt I had regressed — it was almost like I was taking a step forwards and then I was taking two steps back.

Everything was coloured by my depression and the melancholic mind-set at the time, so in reality I was probably making a lot more progress than I could *see*.

The road back to recovery certainly wasn't a straight or simple one — I had to work jolly hard to make any progress at all.

God heals in many different ways — sometimes the sick are instantly healed, sometimes the doctor finds a cure or remedy, sometimes it is a long process of believing and hoping to be healed and also working with a medical team towards your health.

Another of the keys I have discovered through my journey is the importance of both sides of the answer. Because eating disorders are based on "the Lie" (i.e. starting at the lie of *"you are too fat"* and proceeding to every other lie), it is crucial that you are accountable with your recovery to medical professionals who can monitor your recovery — the other side that is necessary is to keep your heart open to God the creator, for He knows us inside out. For me this meant to keep on going to a solid church where God's word was taught, and His presence filled the place, and opportunity was made for people to be saved, healed and set free.

I could have just had the medical help, and I would have been a recovering anorexic all my life. Or I could have just tried to hop in the prayer line and feel God's power on me, there is no disrespect intended — but I wouldn't have had the strength or resilience to contain what He wanted, or even be honest enough to be able to move forward. For me, I needed the two side by side.

Another solution was presented to me early on, and I am sure you have heard this — "Why don't you go to the pastor for counselling?" What a classic! Well for one, we *were* the pastors, and secondly, I would initially get prayer with our district pastors, which was good, but generally I would say, for a very specific problem like this, unless the pastor in question has had a lot of first- hand experience in this area, it is best to get professional help. I would probably not have been able to be completely transparent with (a) someone who knew us, or my parents, or (b) someone who didn't really know about the problem. It would have been too easy to fool them, which wouldn't have helped me in the long run. I always recommend this to people who ask my advice who have or know someone with a similar problem — get a professional to manage the issues, and next to that attend as many church services as possible, and allow the worship to flood over you, so that you can open up to God to allow His healing. God wants to heal us way more than we have any idea how to receive His healing.

I used to feel awkward around some people in the church scene because I was getting psychiatric counselling, as it was something none of us were used to. I often felt like I had this big label on my forehead – "FREAK".

But after a while I came to the conclusion that if I had cancer, I would have gone to an oncologist and not felt like a freak, but would have known that they were the best type of doctor for my sickness. So there was nothing unusual in being treated by a psychiatrist for the anorexia / depression I was suffering.

CHAPTER 17   I KNOW WHAT THIS IS - I GREW UP WITH IT

During the course of me plodding along with my counselling, I went along to church on a particular Sunday morning, and our senior pastors John and Val Lewis had just returned from a long trip which they had taken to various parts of the world.

Pastor Lewis and his wife Val had been to visit many of the churches in revival around the world, including Holy Trinity, Brompton; Ken Gott's church in Sunderland, and the Toronto Airport Church.

When Pastor John got up and spoke that Sunday, something was very different. He did something which at that time was out of the ordinary for the church. He called for anyone who wanted to receive from God a special blessing to come to the front, and to his amazement many of the congregation immediately went forward.

Rich and I both went out to the front. I didn't feel any great bolts of lightning or flashes of fire, but I recognized what this was — I knew it, because I had seen it before. This "New Move of the Holy Spirit" didn't frighten me, nor was I sceptical of it.

As a little girl between five and nine years we had experienced this in our church. Many times the services would go into the wee hours of the morning — people would dance, and laugh, and sing, with a liberating freedom that only comes from the unadulterated presence of God. There was incredible hunger in many of the people, and it brought a real revival atmosphere to our church.

So because I had grown up in this, and known it to be *safe*, I instantly recognized it that Sunday. And although I wasn't well at all in my mind, only my body was healthy at that stage, the one incredible thing that happened to me on that Sunday was the birth of hunger.

That Sunday was the day that I felt my "home" was close — I could start to see things I hadn't seen for years, the many years that had been blurred by dark clouds. I saw through the clouds that Sunday morning, and I knew that even though I wasn't healed I got my *hope* back.

Hope is an incredible force. The Bible says *"Where there is no vision the people perish"*, *"Hope deferred makes the heart sick"*, *"My hope is in the Lord"*, *"Let me not be ashamed of my Hope"*. Hope can help bring the healing.

From that Sunday on I attended every service I possibly could. The church started running special revival services on the Wednesday nights. I would go to as many as I could. I learned to soak in God's presence, and I learned how to receive.

I would go forward for prayer, which was something so foreign to me — I had not allowed many people to pray for me before and I was sceptical of everyone who did. But now I *wanted* to be prayed for, although I never disclosed what I wanted prayer for. I still needed to be safe, and that is really okay, because God knew my problem and I wasn't ready to disclose my heart to the altar workers.

A real hunger was growing. This is not to say I still didn't have the torment and struggle in my daily life — I did struggle greatly. But now there was hope.

CHAPTER 18   RESTORING THE HEART AND THE HOUSE

During this time we had purchased a very old home — a 1925 Federation Home in Queensland. It was a real dump when we bought it, but both of us could see past its ugliness and see the potential for greatness.

It took us two and a half years to transform this ugly duckling into a swan, but in the process I was also being transformed into the beautiful child — body, soul and spirit — that my father God always knew I could become.

The old home had sagging ceilings which needed to be repaired through the attic. Rich and I were both absolutely filthy and completely black when that job was finished. We ripped out the kitchen (which wasn't a kitchen really, just a bench and a sink), and put a lovely timber kitchen in. We went through room by room gap filling and painting. The ceilings were 3.2metres (10' 8" in the old scale), and all the ceilings and walls were tongue and groove. I painted the rooms and stencilled pretty borders, and gradually our daggy house became a nice home.

I began to pour myself out creatively when I was working on the house. I did most of the paintwork, and found it calming to set goals and fulfil them. It was really hard work, but this house was probably the most commented on in the neighbourhood. People would walk past and thank us for restoring "the old house".

Rich and I also put in a beautiful cottage garden in the front with a gorgeous picket fence. I was learning to enjoy beauty again. I planted twenty-nine rose bushes in my garden, so I could constantly have fresh roses on my dining table. I learned the value of enjoyment and spoiling myself with small pleasures such as these.

I also spent many months creating a beautiful candlewick bedspread, which I finally finished and began to use in our old home — this was definitely another of the lessons I learned of simply enjoying life and creating things.

These simple things were an awesome help in diverting me from the monster within. Does this mean I was better instantly? No — I still struggled, but I was learning keys to being a whole person.

A number of years later we sold the house and were to move to another part of Brisbane. The day of the move was incredibly emotional for me. I was tense for most of the day, and when it finally came to leaving, all of our furniture had gone, I was left there mopping the verandah, and the new owner was moving in at the same time. I found it so hard not to cry. I got into the car with my daughter Deb, and cried all the way to the new home. The new home was a much better home for us by far. It was a fairly new brick and tile home with an in-ground pool, so it was better for the family, but I arrived there sure we had just made the hugest mistake of our lives. This was because I had poured out so much emotionally of myself into the old house.

It is vital that we as people have an opportunity to focus on something beyond our own lives and circumstances, and in some way make a difference to something or some area. As restoring this old house helped me, I began again to see

I could do good things, and make a difference to something. Also God the Creator was allowing the creative side of me to be used as part of this journey to wholeness.

CHAPTER 19   THE BIRTHING OF MY NEW LIFE STARTS TO STARVE THE MONSTER'S HOLD

I was on a new journey starting from that Sunday morning when Pastor John and Val returned from their trip, and my hope started growing.

At first I was still a very mentally sick girl, who just happened to be hungry for God's presence.

But there is an amazing thing about hungering after God. It's like you never ever get to the end of it and are satisfied — well not for me anyway. I would experience God's power and presence in my life, and literally see visions of Jesus. One night I had a vision of Jesus in a meadow or field where I was laying down in the grass and He held His hand out to me and wanted me to walk and run through the meadows of flowers with Him. It was beautiful. But an experience like that would never satisfy me, because I have always been an all or nothing person, so I would simply want more.

I had many great moments in God's presence, and I still had to struggle on in my personal life, but the amazing thing I did notice was that the monster's hold was loosening. It was definitely still there but not as strong.

I still had great struggles with depression, but God's healing power was at work in my life.

Part of my healing definitely had to be a choice. It seemed like there were hundreds of days when I wanted to be well, and then I didn't. I would take the healing if I could stay a size six! *But hello — that is not healing girl!*

So part of my healing process was choosing to have as much of God's presence in my life as was possible. This doesn't mean I was instantly healed — because I wasn't instantly healed. Some people just don't stay around long enough to receive their healing. Do you know that healing is just healing — there is no distinction between instant or progressive – the result is the same and the healer is the same — JESUS. Definitely in my life, I know it had to be this way, because God was wooing me and calling me out of death, and I had to CHOOSE LIFE, daily.

CHAPTER 20 STEEL DOORS SLAM SHUT

In May 1995 there was a convention on in Brisbane with a guest speaker from the USA — Rodney Howard-Browne. I actually had no plans to go to this, but coincidentally I saw my parents a few weeks beforehand and they suggested I go to the convention and stay with them in their motel. Rich was happy for me to go, and I felt a bit nonplussed about all of this happening at the last minute, but decided to go.

The week just before this convention, I had one of the worst bouts of depression I had had in months. All I did for three days was lie on the couch — the cloud was so thick that I couldn't even move. However, I still decided to proceed with my plans to go to this convention. I actually had no anticipation that anything extraordinary would happen, except I knew the meetings would be good.

I had never heard this speaker before, and in truth I wasn't attending the meetings to hear him or with any expectation that he would take away my problems. I knew first-hand from growing up as a PK (Pastor's Kid), that that wasn't possible.

The first few days were great — God's word was being taught, we had great worship and there were huge amounts of time devoted to allowing the Holy Spirit to move upon people.

Really for me I was like a sponge that was starting to be filled to saturation point, where any more of God's presence that came upon me just wanted to flood over.

On the Thursday morning there was an awesome and unusual time of worship where God simply filled the place and was tangibly there. Sometime after this a strange thing happened to me. I fell to the ground at the same time as my dad and mum, under the power of God, but what was unusual was that no-one had laid lands on any of us to pray for us. I landed on mum, and she was kind of leaning on dad. It was a most unusual thing, because I remember sensing during that time (around half an hour) that I was being born.

When I got up I still didn't have any lighting flashes or hear God's audible voice, but I felt good on the inside. Also I certainly was hungrier for God than ever before. I don't remember getting up and thinking immediately about my illness, because I know I was thinking about how great God is.

But that moment was the moment when anorexia died in my life. I continued going to every meeting at that conference and I even had the desire to minister to others once again, when that had terrified me for so long, but I wanted God to use me, and knew He would in some way.

Rodney Howard-Browne never called me out for prayer, or had a word of knowledge or any such thing. God the Healer chose to heal me, and He had taught me how to focus on Him, not the prophet, and receive the great present He was trying to give me.

I went away from that convention knowing I was whole. This was something new for me. I never took another anti-depressant tablet. I never spent another day laid out on the couch. I never again struggled with food when I was internally distressed. I was whole — pure and simple — alive and well.

I continued to go to the church meetings as much as possible, and experienced God anew every day.

I had been very faithful with my appointments with Dr Foxcroft my psychiatrist, but had, through different circumstances, missed several months following the conference. However, I returned to see him in August 1995, and I knew this was to be my final visit. He was amazed to see me looking so well, and he then proceeded to talk to me regarding every issue that we had been working on together, one by one, asking me how was this issue, or that issue, and I just said "Great! Brilliant! Fantastic!" Finally he looked at me in a bemused manner and said, "Jo, I don't think you need to see me anymore!" to which I smiled and said, "I already know that. I just wanted to hear you say it".

As I got up to leave his office, I walked out and closed the timber door, but I heard huge 20m high doors of solid steel slam shut, and resound, never to be opened again. I know this was in my spirit's eye, but it was powerful enough for me to still hear them shutting. The illness had no way of sneaking back into my life, because the doors were now finally and completely shut.

It is important to get verification from doctors for healing, even if is to remind yourself, and certain lying symptoms, that God has healed you.

Dear Diary

May

God, today at the Rodney Howard-Browne conference I realised again that I cannot even depend on myself, and you said, "BUT you can depend on ME". Thank you so much.

23rd August

Today was my last visit with Dr Foxcroft — I will never forget it. I am so glad I took the time for this final visit. The sound of those spiritual doors slamming, God — you know I will remember for years and years and so will any who try to accuse me that it isn't finished. God, I pray I remember this sound until I am old and grey.

CHAPTER 21   IT'S TIME FOR PAYBACK

Many of my years had been consumed with this enormous distraction from who I was created to be, so now that I was completely well I wanted the enemy of my soul to know personally – *"You've messed with the wrong person. You will be so sorry that you attacked me, because I am going to help many others get their lives back"*. And this became my catchcry.

But the first time I was called upon me to actually do this, was several months after the convention when I was healed from anorexia, when, one of the pastors from church rang me up late in the afternoon and asked if I would give my testimony at the midweek meeting that night. I answered "Yes", quickly. Although I was filled with all sorts of panicky emotions, I knew I should do this. I guess the scariest thing was that I had kept the whole issue fairly private with 99.9 per cent of the church, so this was a huge step.

The meeting started, and I remember sweating on the moment when I was to share, hoping I would not make some huge blunder. The moment finally came, and before about 400 people I shared what great things God had done and how He had rescued me from myself.

It felt like a blur, but afterwards I felt so elated in knowing I had been obedient. Quick obedience came to be another key factor in my life. I would often say, "Obey quickly before you have time to think about it and talk yourself out of it. Just obey".

From that humble beginning of sharing in our church until now, I have been asked to share this testimony to thousands and thousands of people, and invariably on every occasion that I tell the story, someone will come to me and say, "Thank you for what you have said — I have anorexia or bulimia and need help," or, "My daughter struggles with an eating disorder. What should I do?"

Here is how one amazing story of this lived itself out.   I gave my testimony at the Australian Women's Conference in Adelaide almost 8 years ago. During the course of this conference I was available to help other ministers' wives pray for people down the front who were there for prayer. One young lady named Karen was there whom I did not know, but I was praying for her. She was not a Christian, but was there at the front for prayer because she was moved by my story. I was praying for her, and started sensing things in my spirit, and in my prayers started rebuking and cursing the spirit of eating disorder that was destroying her life. I didn't know anything about her, but simply felt this strongly in my spirit. I didn't hear any more about this until August 2001, (four years later) when I met up with Karen again at another conference I was involved with.

She started relaying the whole story to me, of how she had struggled with an eating disorder for fifteen years. When she came to that conference in Adelaide four years previously she was so amazed at what I had said. Well, God used it to get her attention. She committed her heart to God some time later, and then received her complete healing in January 2001 — and God was awesome enough to arrange for her to meet up with me to tell me about it.

These are the things that I love. I love that, even though I am an imperfect vessel, God loves to breathe through me and totally restore a devastated human being. The key wasn't being perfect, but being willing, ready and able.

For me personally it has been over 10 years of wholeness without one tendency of going back to "death valley", but learning how to walk day by day knowing that Jesus is my personal "Glory, and Lifter of my head".

After several years of doing different things, including pioneering a small church for two and a half years, we made the move to Sydney, to be part of Hillsong Church, in Sydney.

I don't regret the experiences that I have had with anorexia, because through the journey I know I am well on the way to becoming the daughter of the King I was created to be. I may very well have stayed like an ornamental person if I hadn't been broken.

I am determined to live my life the way it was intended, and to cherish the gifts that Jesus entrusted me with. When I will stand before Him one day, my prayer is to see His beautiful smiling face and know that I have pleased Him with I how I used the "GIFT OF LIFE" which He gave me.

I thank you Jesus for trusting me with this – probably the greatest test of my life. You knew even when all hope was gone what the end of my script would read. You knew that I would LIVE TO DECLARE THE GOODNESS OF MY KING!

There is no perfection found in a number on the scales — only in the eyes of the Creator.

Dear Diary

August

*Tonight I have to share my testimony for the first time. God, you showed me the most amazing thing —that you have given me a new headband or title across my forehead – "Beauty for Ashes". This is to replace the title of "Freak" which I have given to myself for ye*ars.

The names you give us are so much more wonderful than the ones we give ourselves.

October

One day in cell meeting we were all praying, and God showed me a vision of Jesus on His throne. He was covered in gold, beautiful beyond any words that I could describe. Then I saw myself. I was no longer miles away from Him, and just part of the throng, but now I was at his feet. After some time I saw myself as a fairy dancer (with no wings, but free like a fairy), with chiffon scarves and a scarf skirt and ballet shoes, dancing uninhibited before Jesus, completely free. Then I saw Jesus enjoying the freedom that He had given me.

God, my prayer is that you would take my flesh and all my weaknesses and burn them up, and you answered me, "I love you and your heart's desire, BUT I set you free from needing to be PERFECT".

November

A friend came over to our house today, and after we ate dinner, we worshipped God and spent time in God's presence. I felt weighed down in your presence Lord — it was actually heavy and painful. Then you said to me, "This is the heaviness of the anointing which I have told you about. But it is still lighter than the burdens that you give to yourself."

CHAPTER 22 THE FAMILY ALBUM

WHAT IS HAPPENING TO MY LOVELY WIFE?

By Richard Luhrs

Everything seemed to be going so well. Jo and I met in Bible College, and were fulfilling our life's passion – pastoring a church. And then this deadly eating disorder appeared which was more than an "ignore it and it will go away" problem. It was a battle, not just for Jo, but for all of us who were close to her. I hope that our story will give you courage and hope in whatever battle you may be facing.

Where did this come from? I can't remember inviting this into our house. This is my description of one very dark night: What a feeling of darkness. I thought I was about to see a corpse behind that locked door. Opening the door I was preparing for the worst, and what did I see? Nobody. The room was empty. I looked in the walk-in robe – not there. I thought Jo must have escaped out of the window, but the window and screen were still in place. I checked the walk-in robe once more and among all the shoes on the floor I saw Jo's feet. Jo was huddled up as small as possible in the corner of the robe, being almost invisible among the hanging clothes. I helped her up and placed her on the bed and sat with her until she fell asleep. That was too close for comfort!

How could this happen? Was it my fault, her fault, her parents' fault, the devil's fault? We were all blamed. We were even asked if we had had sex before marriage. No such luck – to the relief of many of our readers. Isn't it strange that when someone is going through a life threatening situation that some people will try to find out who to blame, while others will try to find out how to help?

Here is how we can help:

❖ seek professional help

❖ continue loving them

❖ believe that they will come through no matter how long it takes

❖ keep your faith in God.

We appreciated the professional help we received but even this was limited — "No one ever fully recovers from anorexia".

I can testify that Jo has fully recovered from anorexia, not one or two weeks ago, but over ten years ago, and so much wants to help others make it through so that they too can be ....Free To Live!

From her loving husband, Rich

PS. I am proud of you honey and so proud of you for writing this book.

DISTANCED FROM MY DAUGHTER

By David Cartledge

Jo-Ann had been the pride and joy of my life from the time she first drew breath. She was always "daddy's girl" and being our only daughter in a houseful of boys guaranteed her special status. Throughout her childhood and teen years there was nothing in her behaviour that ever concerned us. Jo was remarkably compliant and obedient in an environment where her two closest brothers were kicking over the traces, and this gave us needed joy in times when there were plenty of challenges. Even when she was courting Richard she never once came home after the time we expected her or disappointed us in any way.

Her marriage to Richard was like a fairytale, and she inspired us in the early years of their marriage and ministry when they were living far away from us but seemed to cope with the many transitions. We were really blessed by the wonderful work of ministry they had both done in their first solo pastorate at Coolum Beach.

It seemed that they were both increasing in their responsibilities and opportunities with healthy attitudes. Our visits to them were always pleasant and uplifting, so a phone call from Jo while we were in the UK telling us she had been diagnosed with anorexia nervosa was a double shock to me. I had no idea that there was any kind of a problem with her. While recently I had seen a more disciplined side of her than in her youth — for example constant walking over long distances to control her weight — it did not occur to me that this was a symptom of something deeper and more sinister. The second shock was to realize that this was not a minor aberration. To this point any problems had seemed like a bump in the road but this one would not go away, and soon I became aware that this was very likely a life threatening situation. I felt shattered inside – someone I loved with all my heart and would do anything for had become another person without me realizing it, and now she was hard to reach.

On our return to Australia, Marie went immediately to stay with Jo and Richard and to take care of the house and children which Jo was now no longer capable of doing. The daily phone calls from Marie started to confront me with a reality I was not prepared for – our daughter had changed mentally, emotionally and physically. She was desperately ill and may not survive. These combined unpleasant facts crashing on us all at once were hard to cope with. There was still some naive expectation in me that she would wake up one morning soon and everything would be back to normal.

The first time I saw Jo after her illness was diagnosed was at my father's funeral. I met her in the house and tried to hold her close in comfort and reassurance that we were there for her and would do everything possible to see her restored to health and wellbeing. As I held her emaciated body – now nothing but skin and bones — my mind was screaming, *"You will be back here in a month to bury your daughter"*. When I went into the funeral parlour to see my father's body I could hardly focus on him because it seemed to be Jo's face I was seeing and *her* body lying in the coffin. The funeral was a blur to me with the sadness of my father's passing and the certainty that we would soon be at my daughter's funeral.

The issue of Jo's health had become so aggravated that Richard had no choice but to resign from his ministry in order to protect and care for his wife. We supported this wholeheartedly but were still saddened for Richard who was a very good pastor and had done an excellent work at Coolum.

I was not prepared for the emotional onslaught of the next few months. There were times when even our reaching out to her was mistrusted. The things we tried to offer or provide were suspected as attempts to buy her favour. Even our visits were tense, not knowing what strange thing we might be confronted with. Bizarre ideas that she was not a wanted child, or that she and Marie had always had conflict, were stumbling stones to getting our discussions and relationship back onto an even keel. From our perspective none of these things had the slightest element of truth, but they suddenly seemed true to Jo and we did not know how to handle this 'rewriting of history'.

For the next few months our visits and phone conversations were like walking on eggshells. We felt our responsibility was to create a safe and loving environment where Jo could re-discover her joyful roots rather than bring correction of ideas that did not seem rooted in reality. This was the first time in about twenty-eight years that there was any distance between Jo and me. Now it seemed she was unreachable or unstable where even a simple word with a good intent might be misunderstood and become a point of reaction. My heart was struggling to come to terms with this and I was totally unprepared for the new boundaries of our relationship that had been staked out for us by Jo. I was at arms-length with my only daughter and it seemed she wanted it that way. This was not something that could be resolved by conversation or confrontation – only love and patience would pay off. I prayed for her recovery sincerely but realized that this would take more than a trite prayer – we would need to patiently hold the lifeline in faith, hope and love.

There is no question that many thanks are due to her psychiatrist. The weekly visits and medication seemed to restore her to a semblance of stability and normality, but it was still not very satisfying. Jo seemed to live in a fog. Her emotions were blunted and at times she was like a person walking in a trance.

The first real signs of hope occurred in late 1994 when an amazing time of spiritual renewal began occurring at the church Richard and Jo were attending. Something in Jo responded to the worship and waiting in God's presence, and although her body was still in the same state of emaciation her spirit began to lift. Her phone calls to us were now filled with what was happening in the church, and her response to that was having an impact on us as well. Some months later we asked Richard to care for the children while Marie and I took Jo to a national conference of our church, and during those few days a miracle occurred. There was an intense manifestation of the presence of the Lord during one of the conference sessions. Before our eyes we saw a total restoration of Jo's mind and spirit. While it took some time for her body to regain lost weight and stabilize, we had the first signs that our daughter was back from the deep dark abyss that had been her abode for the past few years. Jo told us that during the conference meetings as she was worshipping God, that He took the claw out of her brain! Her psychiatrist discharged her shortly afterward and she needed no more medication. It was a miraculous and immediate recovery from the jaws of death.

She made really rapid progress and showed that she could handle not only the pressures of family life again, but could cope with negative and difficult people without losing her equilibrium or reverting to the lifestyle that brought her to the verge of destruction.

For a number of years following Jo's recovery she managed our ministry office with its busy schedule and the constant unexpected, and was an incredible blessing to both Marie and me. She is dearly loved and respected and we are grateful to God for the miracle that restored our daughter, first to herself, then to her family and to us.

David Cartledge

My Dad went to be with the Lord a short while ago, what has impacted me greatly since his death is that his life was so well lived. His funeral was so impacting, and full of honour, showing many of the great exploits dad had achieved for his God. Dad mentioned in his letter for this book that he thought — and I'm sure many others also thought that my life was about to be tragically cut short by the eating disorder. How heart-rending that would have been — there would have been nothing but trauma and heartache for the family, and as I met my God I would have had nothing but empty hands and pain to bring Him. I'm so grateful to my God that He healed my broken life, and gave me the chance to fulfil the promises He has written over my life, so I may bring Him more than pain and trauma when my race is run.

MY JOURNEY WITH JO

By Marie Cartledge

We were blessed with four beautiful children — three sons and a beautiful daughter Jo-Ann. She was a beautiful child and a great joy to us. Jo grew up to be a wonderful young woman who had one desire and that was to serve God with her life. She was blessed with a brilliant husband, Richard, and eventually had two lovely children of her own — Deborah and Daniel. Our cup was full — they were such a blessing. Being my only daughter, Jo was special to me, and apart from usual differences of opinions during her late teens, we had what I thought was a good mother-daughter relationship. She had a fairy-tale wedding and I don't recall even a moment of tension during the process of the preparations. I was so proud of her.

My husband and I were on an extended holiday overseas when we received a phone message to call Jo urgently. After a lengthy conversation, Jo advised us that she had been diagnosed with anorexia nervosa. This came as a great shock, although I had for some time been concerned about her weight loss, and on the occasions I had mentioned it to her, she did not want to hear what I had to say. Of course I wanted to return immediately to see what I could do to help, as there were two small children to take care of. Jo would not hear of us returning and insisted that we finish out our holiday, which we did.

Upon returning to Australia, I flew immediately to Queensland to stay with her for a month. I was not quite prepared for what I was to see, however Jo was my daughter and I was determined to love her through this, not treat her as a child but just be there to look after the children, Richard and the house.

This was a major crisis in our lives. Jo is our only daughter and now her life seemed to be at an end. However, through other crises that we had faced we had learned that God is our only source — "He is a very present help in time of trouble". I realized that Jo's recovery was going to take time and I made up my mind that however long it took, I would love her, listen to her and be available when she needed me. There was no place for nagging or coaxing or becoming angry with this situation, I was thankful that she was under professional care.

In my own heart, I resolved in my faith that I would not settle for partial recovery in Jo's life — physically or emotionally. So that is what I believed and prayed for during this time of crisis in her life. There were good times and bad times. There were times of feeling that I had lost my daughter — she seemed a stranger to me. However, through it all, I am grateful to be able to say that there is always light at the end of the tunnel. Today Jo is a healthy young woman, wonderful wife, beautiful mother and servant of God, and as her mother I am so proud of her.

I believe that her testimony of faith and courage will enable many who face this type of crisis to be encouraged to believe for a full and complete recovery.

Jo – I love you.

Mum.

CHAPTER 23   MY PASTORS AND FRIENDS HAVE A SAY

PASTOR JOHN LEWIS
Pastor of Northside Christian Family

"I do recall quite vividly the obvious physical effects anorexia had upon Jo's body. She was losing an incredible amount of weight over a relatively short period of time.

I understood the seriousness of the condition and the real possibility of the fatal results. Jo and Richard had taken a forced break from ministry with the intention of allowing Jo to recuperate from her anorexia and during this break they were attending my church.

At the time we were experiencing the powerful visit of the Holy Spirit known as the Toronto Blessing. Jo was so desperate for God — she was open to this new move and took every opportunity to bathe in the presence of the Lord. As we understand now, it was the presence of the Lord for healing.

Over the following months, I witnessed Jo continually prostrated in God's presence and the healing power of Christ working in her physical body.

It was a delight to see her strength renewed and her weight return to normal. Jo was soon restored sufficiently for her and Richard to embark upon pioneering a new church.

I understand Jo has no recurring difficulties with anorexia. I rejoice with Jo and Richard at the wonderful miracle of God's healing power in her body.

Pastor John Lewis

THE STORY OF JO LUHRS

By Lina Cavallaro
Mark and Lina are Senior Pastors at Albany Hills Christian Church

 I first met Jo-Ann in 1980 when Mark and I had decided to go to Rhema Bible College at Calvary Temple in Townsville. Jo went straight from high school to working in the church office. This is where we began to know this beautiful, very reserved and curious girl.

The very first non-traditional wedding we ever went to was that of Richard and Jo-Ann Luhrs. The rituals, vows, dress, reception and crowd were similar to what I was used to in our Italian/Catholic tradition, but this was different! The bride actually sang a song to the groom. It was so romantic that I cried through the whole ceremony. What a privilege it was for our family to be there at this special occasion. We had such a love for this very special family. We just felt privileged to be in close relationship with a family who carried the favour of God and who had Christ as the centrepiece of their lives. This family taught us about faith, how to overcome criticism, and how to "never give up". I wanted to learn as much as I could because one day we would be on the front line in fulltime ministry just like Jo-Ann's mum and dad. Bible College was no theory for me. I watched actions; reactions and I saw the hidden "price tag" of ministry right up front as we worked closely with Jo's family. Without the love of Christ humanity is very cruel, wicked and unmerciful.

Several years later Richard and Jo joined us on our ministry team in our first pioneer work in Singleton, NSW. They had only been married a short while and already had been through a difficult time in Maitland, their first call in ministry. Richard became our youth pastor and Jo took on the role of music director. These were great days of seeing many people become Christians and seeing a church created out of nothing. There was so much growing and learning to do for all of us. Many times the price on the tag was way more than what I expected to pay and at other times it was such a joy that I would even pay more. I still didn't know if a pastor's wife could wear jeans or own an air rifle.

The pressures of demands, late nights with crying babies and the general constant expectations of life began to grow. Coming from a very high achieving family I think it made it even more difficult for Jo to enjoy this season of her life. Richard would get himself aside and pray his way through to the other side. He just seemed to cope with anything but I am sure that he was forced to grow on the inside during this time too.

Deborah and Daniel were two beautiful babies both born in Singleton. Not long after Daniel arrived Richard and Jo moved to pastor their own church in Coolum on the Sunshine Coast in Queensland. I was sad to see them go but at the same time it was great to see them take on this local church, which needed a pastor.

We often kept in touch by mail and the odd contact we had through various occasions. In 1991 we also moved to Brisbane (only a couple of hours from Coolum Beach) and kept in closer contact.

Very quickly I began to notice that Jo was struggling. Although Jo would say that she was allergic to wheat or yeast etc, I knew that her big weight loss was more than that. I began to see that something was seriously wrong with my friend.

So here we were — we knew our good friends were going through a tough time and we knew that we wanted to do something to help. The opportunity came when Richard asked Mark to speak at his church, so we found ourselves going up to the Sunshine Coast. I decided to network with other churches and surgeries in the area and discovered that there was a highly recommended Christian doctor nearby in Brisbane who actually specialized in this area. Without delay I called her and gave a quick overview of Jo's situation and she made a tentative appointment for Jo which we were to try and arrange with Richard and Jo. I knew she was booked out and was rearranging her schedule for this. After reading the books I had bought on eating disorders I was very aware of how people struggling with eating disorders react to other people making decisions for them and telling them what to do. We decided to pay for the initial visit, as the doctor had asked "how can you be sure Jo will come if there is too high a price?"

During the service Mark and I became more and more determined to encourage them to pull back from running the church and to take time out to recover health and family. By the time we arrived at their home for lunch we had a real conviction and determination to stop pretending and being nice with each other and just speak plainly. Lunch was a real game; everything I expected after reading the books happened. Food was a big topic and everything was yummy and even healthy. We all had our plates and ate lunch but it was easy to see that Jo served, moved around, played with small pieces of food and looked busy but did not eat anything substantial. We all kept playing the game. My husband Mark didn't even notice that Jo was not eating anything. Richard knew not to make any comments by now and the children were too little to really know what was happening. When Mark went into the lounge with Richard intending to speak to him about taking a ministry break, I knew it was my time to talk to Jo. "Jo, if I made an appointment with a Christian lady doctor who is highly qualified and comes from a Presbyterian background (not from the Assemblies of God Church), would you go?" I remember being glad that this doctor was not from the AOG, as this gave Jo some privacy. It seemed that there was silence for ages. She just looked at me. At first I thought she was going to be very angry for interfering, and then I thought she might hit me...but then her pain – filled eyes brimmed with tears and she simply said, "Yes". "Well that is great", I said, "because a tentative appointment has been made for tomorrow. Here is the phone number for you to call and confirm the appointment yourself." From then on regular appointments were made.

Very soon afterwards Richard and Jo relocated to the North side of Brisbane. Deborah and Daniel were enrolled in the same school as my sons and we often had coffee or cold drinks when we dropped each other's children off after school. These were great times to connect and have some very deep and meaningful conversations.

There are so many things that I learnt during this challenge my friend went through. One was that unintentionally you, the relative or friend, can actually be part of the problem and not the solution. For example, one day Richard and Jo came by for coffee and Mark made them afternoon tea. Richard had coffee and Jo had a hot milo. I came in from the shops and found Mark piling the cream into Jo-Ann's milo and loading it up with heaps of sugar. I quickly explained to him how fattening food is not the answer. Doing this would make you the enemy for sure. Food and its values are constantly on their mind so sneaking in calories or energy of any kind would not go unnoticed. Anorexia is not about food — it's more about control, identity and punishment. Eating disorders strike at the very core of our existence. You are not worth feeding because you are not worth being alive and taking up space on this earth because you are so not perfect.

Jo-Ann loved to go to revival conferences where the presence of Jesus was very real. This was also part of her healing. We would share revival videos, always looking forward to the next one. It was great to have her dad travelling the world bringing home video copies of revivals that had occurred just days before.

How wonderful it is to see Jo-Ann free from this ugly thing and to see her whole, beautiful and happy in herself and with life. Truly this is a wonderful true story of an Australian woman who faced death face-to-face and has lived to tell her story.

Love Lina

JANET McKEAN
Jo's dearest friend during the time of the illness

Thinking back now, I realise I was (to a degree) was in a state of denial about Jo's condition for quite some time. I kept thinking that she would snap out of it, get over it and get on with life. After all, anorexia is something teenagers suffer from and Jo is a pastor's wife, a mother of two lovely children and the daughter of prominent pastors. I kept thinking she should not be so silly — this was all so childish. Sometime — I can't pinpoint when — it dawned on me that she really did have an eating disorder. We would often share meals together and Jo would either eat every little or nothing at all, or she would disappear after the meal to the bathroom. I realised she was bulimic as well as anorexic. I love my food and I found this hard to comprehend. The strain of the situation began to take its toll on the Luhrs household, with Richard placed under great personal pressure and the children not understanding why mummy wouldn't eat a meal with them. Deborah and Daniel would ask Jo why she wasn't having dinner, and to her credit, she would answer lightly with something like "Mummy's not hungry" or "I ate my dinner earlier". It was a very difficult time. I was watching my best friend slowly starve herself to death while the pain I could see Richard suffering was almost tangible.

Jo would often phone late at night to let off steam and vent her feelings. She would be either angry, upset, depressed or frustrated with the situation. I distinctly remember one phone call that went well into the early hours of the morning. Jo was telling me how little she had eaten over the last week. It seemed to me at the time that she was almost bragging, but I know now that that was not the case. I remember telling her that if she didn't eat she would die. Jo answered "No I won't". I repeated "Jo, if you don't eat, you will die", and once again she answered bluntly, "No I won't". She had lost sight of reality. She seemed to think she was different to everyone else and she could live without food.

When Richard, Jo and the kids packed up and moved to Brisbane so Jo could receive specialist care, I felt as if she had allowed the devil to defeat them. My motives for not wanting them to move were partly selfish. I considered Jo to be my closest friend — someone I could confide in. We didn't even have to say who was calling when we phoned each other and this ugly disease was making them move away.

Why couldn't she just get over it and be able to stay so we could get back to the way we were? I couldn't tell Jo how I felt. She and Richard had enough to deal with. I know they did the right thing and it took a lot of faith and courage for them to "'Give up" their church and ministry and relocate to Brisbane.

We went to visit Richard and Jo a couple of weeks after they moved to Brisbane, and stayed overnight. Richard and my husband, Kieran went out on Saturday afternoon to do "guy stuff" and Jo and I stayed home with the kids. We decided to go for a swim in the pool so we all went and changed into our swimmers. Seeing Jo in her one-piece really brought home to me just how sick she was. I could see every rib and vertebra on her back. Her hip bones protruded and she looked like a skeleton with skin stretched tightly over the bones. Jo still had small "saddle-bags" on her thighs and I thought how amazing it was that with all the starving and weight loss, these were still on the part of her body where she most wanted to lose weight. I found that quite ironic and almost humorous.

When we had our last child dedicated in December 1995, Richard, Jo and the kids came up to Coolum for the day to celebrate the occasion with us. It was then that I saw Jo as God's walking miracle.

She had gained weight, she was happy and contented and God was on the way to restoring unto the Luhrs family, "the years the locusts had eaten". I still miss not having my friend just around the corner. I miss our impromptu meals, but I am so totally blessed that God has healed Jo and her family and the victory is His.

Jo, you are an inspiration. Your steadfastness and dedication (a bit like a pit bull at times!), is truly a blessing to others. Don't give up on what God has placed in your heart. The greatest victory in all this will be seeing God use your testimony to save and heal others. God bless you my dear friend.

Janet

KAREN MURPHY
A wonderful friend of Rich and Jo's, from Coolum

When Jo rang me one night to ask if I would write a letter on our friendship with their family while they lived in Coolum, I felt very privileged. Richard was the pastor of the church we attended, with Jo-Ann his wife, and two very young children then, Deborah and Daniel.

Over the years we became very good friends. Richard was always happy caring for the people in our church and community. They became so much more to us than pastors, they became dear friends. I remember when my husband Trevor and I had just moved into our home — we had a pastoral visit from Richard and he ended up mowing our grass. Trevor and Richard had a great time as they developed a friendship of continual joking around.

Jo was a very dedicated wife and mother, and what was so special about her was her gift of hospitality. I remember many great times around a meal at their home, with our children playing together. We always felt welcomed.

It was during these years that Jo-Ann suffered increasingly from an eating disorder, but because of Richard's cheerfulness and Jo-Ann's quietness, it wasn't really obvious to us that the suffering in their home was leading to a crisis in their lives.

It was when they decided to leave Coolum and start a new chapter in their lives, that we realised the seriousness of the problem. It was a big shock to us when they decided to leave and we missed them so much. From time to time we were able to visit them and we could see that Jo-Ann was slowly over-coming the problem, through her faith, and with help from her powerful loving God and the support of her devoted family.

Karen

CHAPTER 24 THE DOCTOR'S REPORT

DR CAROLYN RUSSELL
Carseldine Medical Centre

Dr Carolyn Russell - MBBS, Dip RACOG, RACGP

Dr Russell is a practicing GP with 20 years experience, a Fellowship of RACGP and a postgraduate counselling degree. She is Principal of the Carseldine Medical Centre, which runs a Complex Conditions Clinic.

Carolyn is an experienced communication skills educator and tutors at the University of Queensland Centre for General Practice.

Dear Jo,

Thank you for the opportunity to read the draft of your book. I was delighted to hear of your ongoing life in the Lord and His continued support in your life and the growth you are experiencing. I am very happy to write a few words of support.

Anorexia Nervosa is one of the most confusing and destructive conditions known to the medical profession and those affected both patients and their families. It affects many young people at the time when their lives are just beginning, steals away years of some people's lives and as well, severely disrupts relationships in their families.

When I first met Jo and her husband, the effects of the illness were very obvious in her physical and emotional state, and the secondary family traumas were starting. They were leaving a ministry post after finally acknowledging the presence of the insidious anorexia in their midst. Jo describes very well the struggle to finally face this truth.

It is wonderful now to read her book where she writes with such great honesty of the struggle to understand, to accept the work necessary to stop the effects of the condition, and to face some issues which were very painful in her history. To read of this and the growing work of the Lord Jesus Christ in her life over the following years encourages me to continue to walk with people suffering the effects of this devastating condition, and to look forward to healing being seen in their lives also.

A miracle really does occur when we come to trust the Saviour who was given to us by God to show us the truth. Sometimes this same miracle seems to come more slowly as we honestly face illness and pain, and learn the lessons that these experiences can teach us.

Jo is a living example of one of these miracles as she faces each day in the promised love of Christ who cares for her, and learns to live in that certainty.

I look forward to reading more chapters of her life story in the future.

Regards to you all

Carolyn Russell

CHAPTER 25   MERCY MINISTRIES

Mercy
Ministries

I am grateful every day for the miracle that God gave me – life and hope and the courage to continue the journey. I know that I am only one of God's miracles. He loves to restore His children and make broken lives whole. He restores dignity where it has been stolen and makes the impossible possible in many lives across the world.

"I'll show up and take care of you as I promised and bring you back HOME, I know what I'm doing. I have it all planned out – plans to take care of you, not abandon you, plans to give you the FUTURE you hope for. When you call on me, when you come and pray to me, I'll listen. When you come looking for me, you'll find me. Yes, when you get serious about finding me and want it more than anything else, I'll make sure you won't be disappointed". Jeremiah 29:11 (The Message)

I want to give honour to a wonderful ministry called Mercy Ministries. Their sole purpose for being is allowing God to use them to rescue and restore young women suffering from eating disorders, depression, self-harm, unplanned pregnancy, abuse, addictions, obsessive or compulsive issues and suicidal tendencies. Mercy has two homes in the United States, two Homes in Australia and, plans for a home in New Zealand and in each State of Australia in the near future.

Mercy Ministries was founded twenty years ago by Nancy Alcorn, who had personal experience of working in government institutions for hurting girls. God has used Nancy incredibly to help rescue and restore thousands of girls. I believe in the principle that when you are diligent with what is in your hand God trusts you with more, as He knows you will care for it. That certainly has been the case for Nancy, as the first home in Louisiana, which opened in 1983, was not large enough to cater for all the girls that needed help, so a second home was opened in Nashville in 1996.

In May 2001 the first Australian home was opened in Sydney, which has grown incredibly, and the need was still so great that a second home was opened on the Sunshine Coast in January 2003.

Mercy provides a residential program that is free of charge to the girls during their stay which is on a voluntary basis. The program is known around the world for its ability to combine God's unconditional love and transforming power with professional counselling and care.

The environment is extremely encouraging, as opposed to the depressing atmosphere of many institutions where these girls may have previously been.

The homes are beautiful, and they are furnished to help the girls understand that they are truly princesses. There is no sterile atmosphere at all but a wonderful colourful environment.

Each young woman participates in class time, household tasks, recreation and counselling. Every day there are studies (bible studies, life skills, and general life studies) which the girls attend, which is a great foundation for allowing the scriptures to become real to the girls in their different circumstances.

Mercy is a new beginning for thousands of girls. Once the girls have completed their program, which is set out between them and the counsellor, Mercy puts on a special graduation ceremony where family and friends are invited to celebrate the miracle of their lives restored.

Melissa B

I have included two wonderful stories of restoration from some girls who have been through the Mercy program in Australia.

The word I would use to describe myself was tormented. I was completely disillusioned with life, hated myself and hated God for giving me a life I didn't ask for and didn't want. For over ten years I had struggled with anorexia, and as tormented as I was, part of me loved it. It gave me a real sense of fulfilment in life like nothing I had ever known. It was what I lived for. I was obsessed with exercise and couldn't allow myself to rest or sit still. To complicate matters, as anorexia got a deeper hold on me, my obsessive tendencies grew and I developed obsessive compulsive disorder. This took on a life of its own and overtook my mind and my life. I was terrified of being around food and calories of any sort, fearing that I could gain weight if I was near them. I couldn't take that risk. I felt like the whole world was contaminated and the only place I could find peace was to shut myself in my room. Some days I would be washing my face, hands and body for six hours to put my fears at rest. Even things I love, like going shopping had lost any joy.

My world became so small and there was no room for life in it. I came to a point where I couldn't take care of myself. At a time in my life where I was supposed to be getting my career established and out enjoying life, I was completely tormented and wanting to end it all. Over the years I'd been to see many professionals; psychiatrists, psychologists, dieticians and counsellors. There were improvements but no lasting change, and things would eventually slip back to the way they were. Deep down I knew God was the answer and I hung on to the scripture, "God is faithful, He will not let you be tempted beyond what you can bear but when you are tempted He will also provide a way out so that you can stand up under it". (1 Cor 10:13). Mercy has been my way out. The decision to come to Mercy was not easy, but I knew I was incapable of stopping this destructive behaviour on my own. I had to hand over my need to control food and address the underlying issues. At Mercy, staff have shown me how to combat my fears with God's word, replacing the lies with His truth.

Mandy

I left my gang to come to Mercy. The night before I came to Australia, my friend was killed because she wouldn't tell them where I was. My choices didn't just affect me, but people that I loved and cared about. Since coming to Mercy I am daily replacing the lies with the truth — I am not the same girl.

When I talked to people, I talked to their shoes. It took me four months to let anybody hug me. Those are the two major things that come to mind, but it's the things God has done inside that have really made the difference. Every day I am faced with choices — they can be the smallest things like making my bed or keeping my room tidy, or bigger things like not carrying on the destructive patterns of the past. I now understand that choices have consequences, and I'm not perfect, but I'm daily walking out the best possible choices for my life. I thank God for Mercy, because without Mercy I wouldn't be here today.

Mercy Ministries is supported entirely by contributions from church groups, individuals and corporations. If you would like to contribute or partner with Mercy Ministries to help more young women in desperate need please phone toll free 1800 011 537 (Australia) or 615-831-6987 (USA) to find out how you can help.

If you are in need of help, maybe your story is similar to mine, I highly recommend Mercy Ministries to you. They can set you on the path to Hope, and Healing.

For more information about Mercy Ministries contact

Website

www.mercyministries.com

www.mercyministries.com.au

www.mercy.net.nz

Or phone toll free

Australia   1800 011 537

USA   615-831-6987.

CHAPTER 26   WHERE TO FROM HERE?

My hope for you is that if you are reading this book and you are in need of a *Miracle* whether your life is similar to my story or not, never forget that our God is in the Miracle working business. He loves to restore and heal and save and deliver. His *Heart* is for you. He *B*elieves in *You*. He created you, and if you need a miracle – there is *N*othing that is too hard for Him.

So when I am thinking of where to from here? *for you,* I hope this may begin your journey to *H*ope, *L*ight, *L*ife and *F*reedom and *B*eauty. I pray that you will find freedom if you are held prisoner, or healing if you are sick. But most of all I pray that you find *Jesus* – because in Him all your questions will be answered – He is our *Hope.*

For myself, *my journey continues.* I am the beautiful daughter of a Wonderful Heavenly Father – who knew me before I was born and knew that I would be able to stand in this battle, and in the battles to come to declare His Life and Liberty to other captives He so desperately wants to set free.

I thank God for giving my *Life* back to me, not just so I could be selfish and enjoy that life, as wonderful as it is, but so I can, with His help go beyond myself and my comfort zone to be a *Light* in a very dark place — to help those who don't know how to ask for help, to be a carrier of His anointing power to break the chains of death and destruction, and believe with you for *Miracles.* I love you and believe in you.

For Jesus   Thank you for leaving your heavenly home, so beautiful with streets of gold, to come down to my broken world, and give me a *Chance* to *Live.*

www.ingramcontent.com/pod-product-compliance
Lightning Source LLC
Chambersburg PA
CBHW062220080426
42734CB00010B/1964